BUNDU FOOD

for the African Bush
Rita van Dyk

Acknowledgements

A special thank you to everyone who shared their recipes with me and to Johan and Concha for being such eager guinea pigs and enthusiastic tasters. I would also like to extend an extremely well deserved thank you to Nelia Richter of *DriveOut* magazine for all her help and invaluable advice.

Published in 2013 by Struik Lifestyle
(an imprint of Random House Struik (Pty) Ltd)
Company Reg. No 1966/003153/07
Wembley Square, Solan Road, Cape Town 8001
South Africa
PO Box 1144 Cape Town 8000 South Africa

www.randomstruik.co.za

Reproduction by Hirt & Carter Cape (Pty) Ltd
Printing and binding by 1010 Printing
International Ltd, China

Publisher: Linda de Villiers
Managing editor: Cecilia Barfield
Design manager: Beverley Dodd
Editor & indexer: Anja Grobler
Designer: Beverley Dodd
Photographer: Warren Heath
Stylist: Lisa Clark
Stylist's assistant: Sara Lohmaier
Proofreader: Joy Clack (Bushbaby Editorial Services)

ISBN 978 143230 184 2

Contents

Kitchen packing list 4

Ten-day menu in the bush 7

Breakfast 10

Soups 22

Fish and seafood 28

Chicken 36

Meaty mains 50

Sauces 88

Pastas 94

Vegetarian mains 102

Vegetables 110

Salads 120

Sides 130

Breads and bakes 136

Desserts 144

Index 158

Conversion table 160

Kitchen packing list

The aim of this packing list is not to cart along everything that appears on the list. Rather view it as a guide that you can use to choose things that you are likely to need on your travels. Your motto should be: "Pack as little as possible without inconveniencing yourself". The only thing worse than forgetting an essential item is having to unpack for 2 hours simply to get to the egg lifter. Add items to the list that you would not be able to do without.

It's always a good idea to go on a camping weekend before you embark on a major safari. This will give you the opportunity to identify those items that you need as well as unnecessary items. Everyone's needs differ. You may dislike drinking coffee out of a tin mug while the next person sees this as an integral part of the safari experience.

Always check what the rules and regulations are in terms of food and alcoholic beverages when you are travelling to a neighbouring country.

The hardware

- ammo boxes
- apron
- bottle opener
- camping/fold-out chairs
- can-opener
- cast-iron pot
- corkscrew
- basin
- bottles (for milk, juice and water)
- braai dish
- braai fork
- braai grid
- braai skottel
- braai tongs
- braai tripod
- braai wood or briquettes
- breadboard

- bubble wrap
- cheese cutter
- cling wrap
- coffee pot
- colander
- cool box
- cutlery
  - bread knife
  - forks
  - knife sharpener
  - knives
  - meat knife
  - pocket knife
  - salad spoons
  - serving spoons
  - tablespoons
  - teaspoons
  - vegetable knife
  - vegetable peeler

  - wooden spoons
- cutting board
- dishes
  - marinating dish
  - pudding dish
  - salad bowl
  - serving dishes
- egg lifter
- fire lighters
  - cigarette lighter
  - matches
- foil
- folding table
- fridge
- fruit container
- frying pan
- gas burner (normal)
- gas burner (steak plate)
- gas cylinder

- gas cylinder attachments
  - gas bottle extension
  - gas key(s) arm
- glasses (cold drink and wine)
- grater
- grid brush
- hand mixer or whisk
- headlamp
- headlamp batteries
- hiking stove
- ice bags
- jaffle pan
- jerry cans for water
- kebab skewers
- kettle (fire/gas)
- measuring cups
- measuring spoons
- milk jug
- mosquito net
- mugs for coffee, tea
- oven gloves/welding gloves
- pans
- plastic bags (large and small, for leftovers)
- plastic containers (different sizes, with lids)
- plates
- paper plate holders
- paper plates
- porridge and pudding bowls
- potato masher
- pot holder
- recipe books
- rubber bands (to seal open bags of sugar, etc.)
- sauce brush

- saucepans
- scissors
- screw-top containers
- serviette holder
- serviettes
- table cloth (fabric and/or plastic)
- teapot
  - strainer (tea leaves)
- toothpicks
- trays
- vacuum flask(s)
- water container with tap

In the food chest

- baking powder
- bicarbonate of soda
- biltong
- biscuits: sweet and savoury
- Bisto
- bottled sauces
- bread
- bread rolls
- breakfast cereal
- bully beef
- butter/margarine
- canned products
  - beans
  - creamed sweet corn
  - fruit
  - ham
  - mussels
  - tomato-and-onion mix
  - tomatoes
  - tuna

  - vegetables
  - whole kernel corn
- cheese
- chickpeas
- Chinese rice noodles
- chocolate
- chutney
- cocoa
- coffee
- cold drinks
- cold drink powder
- condensed milk
- cooking oil
- curry powder
- couscous
- custard powder
- desiccated coconut
- dried fruit
- dried vegetables
- dried sausage (*droëwors*)
- eggs
- fish
- flour
  - bread flour
  - cake flour
  - cornflour
  - self-raising flour
- fresh fruit
- fresh vegetables
- fruit juice
- gherkins
- grains
- herbs and spices
- honey
- ice
- Ideal milk

- instant mash
- instant pudding
- instant sauce
- instant soup
- instant yeast
- jam
- jelly powder
- lemon juice
- liquor
- long-life cream
- long-life custard
- long-life milk
- mayonnaise
- mealie meal
- meat
- milk powder
- Milo
- mustard (powder and prepared)
- Nestlé Caramel Treat
- nuts
- oats
- olive oil
- olives
- pasta
- peanut butter
- pesto
- pickled onions
- polenta
- popcorn
- potato chips
- raisins
- rice
- rusks
- salad dressing
- soup (packets and canned)
- soy sauce
- Spray and Cook
- spreads (Marmite, fish paste etc.)
- stock cubes
- sugar
- sweets
- syrup
- Tabasco
- tea
- Thai noodles
- tomato paste
- tomato purée
- tomato sauce
- vinegar
- water
- Worcestershire sauce
- yoghurt

In the cleaning box

- bleach (Jik)
- bottle brush
- broom and dustpan
- bucket with lid
- cloths
- dish cloths
- dishwashing brush
- dishwashing liquid
- Handy Andy
- nailbrush
- newspapers
- paper towels
- pot scourers
- rubbish bags
- rubbish bin
- scouring sponges
- soap
- sponges
- steel wool
- washing basin plugs
- washing up basin(s)
- washing up cloths
- wet wipes

Ten-day menu in the bush

It's easy feeding a group of people on safari if they don't mind eating bully beef on Cream Crackers morning, noon and night. But if they have more sophisticated palates, or are simply fussy eaters, then you have got your work cut out for you. Hopefully this menu for 10 days in the bundu will help.

Remember, the lists are not the be-all and end-all; add a good dash of common sense and adapt them to your needs. For example, there's meat on the packing list, but if you're travelling to a neighbouring country that has meat restrictions, you'll need to make a separate list and buy the meat there. Or, say, if you need to drive really far on the fourth day of your holiday and you'll only arrive at your destination quite late, you need to ensure that the menu for that day has a supper that can be whipped up in a jiffy. It's definitely not a night for a potjie. It is possible to buy fresh bread, veggies and fruit out in the sticks, but the golden rule is always to be self-sufficient. If you're unsure whether you'll find certain foodstuffs at your destination, rather plan ahead and take them along, or take the ingredients to make them.

Whatever the case may be, the 10 pantry items without which you shouldn't even think of going on safari, are standard:

- salt
- oil
- flour (cake flour for bread and *vetkoek*, and mealie meal for porridge)
- milk (preferably long-life milk, or powdered milk)
- onions
- potatoes
- tomatoes
- eggs
- pasta
- sugar

Day 1

Breakfast: Coffee and rusks.

Lunch: *Padkos* you've made at home, such as hard-boiled eggs, meatballs, *sarmies* (sandwiches) with apricot jam and a flask of coffee or tea.

Supper: Matured rump steak; garlic bread in foil (make it at home and wrap it in a plastic bag so that the cool box doesn't reek of garlic for the rest of the trip); mixed salad.

Dessert: Blocks of chocolate.

Day 2

Breakfast: Bacon or bully beef; eggs; tomatoes; toast.

Lunch: Cheese sandwiches (made that morning at camp); yoghurt and fresh fruit.

Supper: Sausage (*boerewors*) (cook enough for breakfast the next day); *mieliepap* (porridge made from mealie meal); tomato salad; whole, cooked beetroot.

Dessert: Fruit salad (make enough for tomorrow's lunch; slice in the bananas just before you eat it so that they don't go brown).

Day 3

Breakfast: *Boerewors*; scrambled eggs; toast; can of beans in tomato sauce.

Lunch: Salami-and-cheese sandwiches (made at camp in the morning); fruit salad.

Supper: Pasta with bolognaise sauce; mixed salad.

Dessert: Canned peaches with long-life cream.

Day 4

Breakfast: Oats with raisins, honey and milk; yoghurt.

Lunch: Bully beef or canned ham, sliced on wholewheat bread; gherkins.

Supper: Chicken-and-vegetable curry; rice; cucumber sambal; tomato-and-onion sambal; banana slices with sweet sauce.

Dessert: Trifle.

Day 5

Breakfast: French toast; stewed fruit with honey and cinnamon.

Lunch: Watermelon or *spanspek* skewered on kebab skewers with blocks of feta cheese in between; cheese; mussels; Portuguese sardines; savoury crackers.

Supper: Lamb-shank *potjie* (it takes 3 hours to cook soft, so make it on a day that you're at camp early); rice; stuffed butternut; quartered tomatoes.

Dessert: Brown pudding with long-life custard.

Day 6

Breakfast: Toasted cheese sarmies, fried in the pan (or add your favourite filling).

Lunch: Tuna mayo sandwiches; packet of three-bean salad.

Supper: Vegetable soup; Portuguese butterflied chicken, grilled over the coals; couscous; diced cucumber and dates.

Dessert: Roast pineapple with long-life cream or ice cream.

Day 7

Breakfast: Bread rolls; frankfurters; eggs.

Lunch: Canned ham, sliced; potato salad; freshly chopped cabbage, mixed with a bottle of curried beans.

Supper: Lamb chops and *sosaties*; *mieliepap*; pumpkin pie; whole head of cabbage in foil.

Dessert: Pear halves filled with instant chocolate mouse.

Day 8

Breakfast: Sweet-corn fritters with syrup; bacon (save some for the avocado salad at lunchtime); fried eggs.

Lunch: Avocado halves filled with bacon bits, small pieces of raw cauliflower and mayonnaise; savoury crackers.

Supper: Steak; vegetables in foil parcels (potato, butternut, sweet potato, etc.).

Dessert: Dumplings.

Day 9

Breakfast: One-pot breakfast (bully beef, tomatoes, onions and chunks of cooked potato).

Lunch: Tortillas filled with grated cheese, tomato, salami and mayonnaise; apples that have been cored and filled with raisins mixed with chunky peanut butter.

Supper: *Boerewors* (braai enough so that there are leftovers for lunch the next day); mashed potatoes; canned peas, sweetened with sugar; tomato salad.

Dessert: Banana flambé with long-life cream.

Day 10

Breakfast: Cereal (it's easy, with minimal washing up) or boil a few eggs and save some for lunch.

Lunch: Leftover *boerewors*; boiled eggs; mini *vetkoek* (make them the previous evening).

Supper: Grab takeaway pizzas the moment you've unhitched your trailer.

Breakfast

Quiche in a tin cup
Serves 1

*Because you can use any ingredients with this recipe –
fried bacon, asparagus, ham, tomato, salmon and even
vegetables – you can dream up endless variations.*

2 eggs
1/4 cup milk
salt and pepper to taste
extra ingredients, such as bacon, feta, mushrooms
   and chopped, cooked sausages
butter or margarine to grease the tin cup

Place a large pot of water on a gas stove and fire it
up. Ensure that the cup you're going to use fits into the
pot – the water should come about halfway up the sides
of the cup. Beat the eggs, milk and seasoning together,
and add the extra ingredients to taste. Grease the cup
thoroughly to ensure that the cooked quiche will slip out
easily later. Pour the mixture into the cup and place the
cup into the boiling water. Cover the pot with a lid and
let it boil for about 10 minutes, or until the egg is cooked.
Run a knife around the edge of each quiche every now
and then to loosen it. Also press the quiche softly with
the back of a spoon so that the raw egg can run from the
middle to the sides. But don't be too rough with it, as
the quiche could break. When you remove the cup, run
a knife around the edge of the quiche again to loosen it.
Then put a plate over the cup and quickly tip it over so
the quiche can slip out. Or eat it directly from the cup.

Bully beef and eggs
Serves 4

*Bully beef is enjoyed by one and all, just give it a try,
I promise you will not be disappointed.*

1 onion, peeled and chopped
2 tablespoons oil
1 x 300 g can bully beef
5 eggs
1/4 cup milk
salt and pepper to taste (not too much salt as the
   meat is already salty)
4 slices toast

Fry the onion in half the oil (1 tablespoon) until golden
brown. If you prefer, remove the fat from the bully beef
and then add it to the onion. Use a fork to spread, loosen
and combine the bully beef and the onion. Beat the eggs,
milk and salt and pepper together. In a separate pan, heat
the remaining oil and make scrambled eggs. Spoon the
bully beef onto the toast and place the scrambled eggs
on top.

Eggs in a hole
Serves 2

This recipe is so easy that even the most inexperienced cook can make it.

2 slices bread
1 tablespoon butter
2 eggs
salt and pepper to taste

Make a hole in the bread with a glass or a cup. Melt half of the butter in a pan and place the first slice of bread in it. Break an egg into the hole, place the lid on the pan and bake until done. Season to taste, remove from the pan and keep warm. Repeat the above method with the second slice of bread and egg. The eggs and bread taste even better if fried in bacon fat.

Tip: It saves time to have a pan that is big enough to make both the portions simultaneously.

Bread wheels
Serves 2

If you are planning to take to the road before the sun is up, prepare these sandwiches the night before. They are the perfect coffee companions when having breakfast next to the road.

4 slices bread, crusts removed
4 tablespoons smooth cottage cheese, cream cheese or cheese spread
4 tablespoons finely grated biltong
cling wrap
kebab skewers

Flatten each slice of bread slightly by rolling with a clean bottle or can. Try not to break the bread. Spread the cheese evenly over each slice and sprinkle the biltong over. Roll up each slice and wrap it tightly with cling wrap. Place in the freezer for 30 minutes. Remove the cling wrap and slice the rolls thickly so that they look like wheels.

Frittata
Serves 4

A scrumptious breakfast that everyone will enjoy.

3 tablespoons oil
1 large potato, peeled and thinly sliced
5 eggs
salt and pepper to taste
2 medium tomatoes, diced OR 8 rosa tomatoes, quartered
$1/2$ cup grated Cheddar cheese

Heat the oil in a pan and fry the potato slices until brown and done. Remove the potato slices from the oil, drain on paper towels and set aside. Beat the eggs with a fork and season to taste. Pour the egg mixture into the previously used pan, cover with a lid and cook over medium heat without stirring. Lift the edge of the eggs now and then with an egg lifter and tilt the pan to allow the raw egg to run in under the cooked part. While the top is still slightly runny, distribute the tomatoes evenly onto the eggs. Place the potatoes on top and season to taste. Sprinkle the cheese over and let it bake for another minute with the lid on so that the potatoes can warm through and the cheese can melt. Loosen the frittata with an egg lifter and slide it onto a plate. Cut into quarters and serve with toast.

Caramelised onions
Serves 2

If you thought onions couldn't possibly be a meal on their own, think again! Serve these caramelised onions as a light meal with toast or French toast, or use it as a jaffle filling.

1 tablespoon olive oil
3 large onions, peeled and thinly sliced
3 tablespoons soft brown sugar
3 tablespoons balsamic vinegar
salt and pepper to taste

Heat the oil in a pan over medium heat. Fry the onions until soft. Add the brown sugar and vinegar and season to taste. Let the onions simmer uncovered for about 15 minutes, stirring often until they have caramelised.

Sausage stew

Serves 6–8

If you want to save time, you can fry the boerewors and cook the potatoes the night before you plan to serve the stew.

2 tablespoons oil
1 kg boerewors, cut into short pieces
2 onions, peeled and chopped
1 garlic clove, peeled and chopped
$1/2$ sweet pepper, seeded and diced
12 cooked baby potatoes, peeled (or 3 large potatoes, peeled
   and cubed)
3 medium-sized tomatoes, peeled and diced (or 1 x 400 g can
   tomatoes, diced)
$1/2$ teaspoon chilli flakes (optional)
3 tablespoons Worcestershire sauce
salt and pepper to taste

Heat the oil in a deep pan or flat-bottomed *potjie* and fry the sausage until brown and done. Remove and drain on paper towels. If there is a lot of oil in the pan, pour most of it off so that only a little remains. Fry the onions and garlic in the remaining oil until the onions are golden brown. Add the remaining ingredients, including the sausage, and simmer for 10 minutes with the lid on. Sausage stew tastes especially good with baked eggs and *mieliepap*.

Mexican eggs
Serves 3

This is the perfect breakfast to serve to your vegetarian friends.
Just make sure that they do eat eggs and cheese as some vegetarians
do not eat any animal by-products.

3 tablespoons oil
1 onion, peeled and chopped
1 garlic clove, peeled and chopped
1 sweet pepper, seeded and diced (preferably a red
    sweet pepper, but a green or yellow one will do)
2 medium-sized tomatoes, diced (or $1/_2$ x 400 g can tomatoes, diced)
1 teaspoon dried oregano
1 teaspoon dried basil
1 teaspoon sugar
2 bay leaves
3 eggs
salt and pepper to taste
2 tablespoons chunky cottage cheese or $1/_2$ cup feta cheese blocks
2 teaspoons basil pesto

Heat the oil in a large pan. Fry the onion and garlic until the onion is
soft. Add the sweet pepper, tomatoes, oregano, basil, sugar and bay
leaves. Cover and simmer for 10–15 minutes over low heat. If the
sauce is too dry, just add a little boiling water. Make three wells in the
sauce using the back of a spoon. Break an egg into each well, put the
lid back on and bake the eggs until cooked to taste. Season to taste.
Dish up from the pan onto slices of toast and top with the cottage
cheese and basil pesto.

Scotch eggs

Makes 4 eggs

Scotch eggs are the best padkos imaginable. Make a few extra – you'll only have crumbs left.

6 pork bangers, cut open, meat removed
1 tablespoon dried parsley or use fresh parsley if you're
    making it at home
1 teaspoon dried chives or fresh chives
a pinch of salt and pepper (the bangers usually have enough salt)
4 hard-boiled eggs, shells removed
$^1/_2$ cup cake flour
1 egg, beaten
1 cup fine, dried breadcrumbs
oil for deep-frying

Mix the pork, parsley, chives and seasoning together and divide into four equal portions. Press each portion flat in your hands until it's big enough to cover an egg. Roll each hard-boiled egg in cake flour and place onto the meat covering. Cover the eggs in the pork mixture and make sure they're sealed properly (no part of the egg should remain uncovered). Dip the covered egg in the beaten egg and then roll it in the breadcrumbs. Heat the oil until moderately warm and fry the Scotch eggs in the oil until golden brown all over. Drain the eggs on paper towels and let them cool before stowing them in the cool box. Cut each Scotch egg in half before serving. Keep a paper serviette at hand to wipe up the crumbs.

Tip: Unlike standard boiled eggs, you can store the Scotch eggs in the fridge overnight; they will still be perfectly tasty if you make them the night before your early-morning start.

Poached egg in cling wrap

Serves 1

It's unlikely that this recipe will propel you through to the final stage of MasterChef, but not everyone can make a poached egg. This method makes it easy to prepare a poached egg in the bush and it cannot possibly flop!

cling wrap
a cup, mug or glass
1 egg

Bring a pot of water to the boil. While you are waiting for the water to heat up, place a large sheet of cling wrap over the cup. Push the cling wrap to the bottom of the cup with a wooden spoon so it forms a hollow into which you can break the egg. Break the egg into the cup and twist the cling wrap to seal it tightly, but leave a little space so the egg can expand. Remove the bag from the cup and place it in the rapidly boiling water for 7–10 minutes, depending on how soft you prefer your egg. Allow for a piece of cling wrap to hang over the side of the pot to make it easier to remove the egg when done. Remove the cling wrap from the water, leave to cool and use scissors to cut open and remove the egg.

Tip: You could make more than one poached egg at a time, just ensure that the pot is big enough for all the eggs to fit comfortably.

Boiled bush omelette

Serves 1

This is not how Nigella Lawson would make an omelette, but what does she know about cooking in the bush anyway? Besides, it's healthy, because it contains no oil or butter.

2 eggs
$^1/_4$ cup milk
extra ingredients, such as sliced ham, cheese, green pepper and fried bacon
salt and pepper to taste

Fill a pot halfway with water and bring to the boil. Beat the eggs and milk together, add your preferred extra ingredients, season to taste and pour the mixture into a medium-sized Ziploc® bag. Squeeze all the air out of the bag and seal it. Place the bag into the boiling water and let it simmer for 10–13 minutes. Remove the bag from time to time (be careful, it's hot!) and carefully squeeze the mixture with your hands (wear oven gloves or use a tea towel), so the cooked and raw egg can mix. When the omelette is cooked, roll it out of the bag and serve with toast.

Soups

Pea soup
Serves 6–8

Why would you serve pea soup from a can when it is so incredibly easy to make this tasty, filling and wholesome soup yourself? Homemade food is always tastier than the shop-bought counterpart.

1 x 250 g packet rindless bacon, diced
1 x 500 g packet split peas
1 small onion, peeled and finely chopped
2 carrots, peeled and diced
1 potato, peeled and diced
1 beef stock cube, dissolved in 1 cup boiling water
7 cups boiling water
salt and pepper to taste

Fry the bacon, without butter or oil, in a large pot and stir continuously so it doesn't burn. As soon as the bacon is done, add the peas, onion, carrots, potato, beef stock and water. Simmer over low heat for 1 hour, stirring often to stop it from catching. Drain the mixture and set the liquid aside for later use. Mash the peas with a potato masher. The bacon won't mash up completely, but it gives the soup a nice texture. Add the drained liquid to the soup mixture and stir through. Add a little water if the soup is too thick for your liking. Season to taste. Put the pot back onto the stove or over the coals to warm through. Serve with bread.

Variation: To save time you could replace the split peas with 1 x 500 g packet frozen peas (reduce the water to 4 cups). The soup will then cook much faster because the peas won't take as long to soften, but frozen peas take up valuable space in your camp-freezer.

Watermelon gazpacho

Serves 4

Is there anything better than some cold watermelon on a hot summer's day? This cold soup is the perfect watermelon alternative and even those who do not normally like cold soup will love this watermelon treat!

5 cups pitted and diced watermelon
1 x 200 ml can tomato cocktail
$^1/_4$ teaspoon chilli flakes
salt and pepper to taste
1 small ripe tomato, peeled and diced
1 tablespoon diced green or yellow or red pepper
1 tablespoon peeled and diced red onion
1 tablespoon diced cucumber

Using a wooden spoon, press and rub 3 cups of watermelon through a fine sieve into a bowl. When making this at home, use a blender to finely chop up the watermelon. Chop up the remaining watermelon (2 cups) into small pieces, add to the fine watermelon and stir through. Add the tomato cocktail and chilli flakes, season to taste and stir through. Refrigerate the soup in your camp fridge. In a separate bowl, mix together the remaining ingredients and refrigerate. When serving, first ladle the watermelon soup into a bowl and then place some of the vegetable mixture in the middle of each soup bowl.

Tip: To chop the watermelon into small pieces, place it in a cup or mug and chop it inside the cup with a knife.

Easy prawn soup

Serves 6

If someone in your safari group is allergic to shellfish, you can replace the prawns with chunks of cooked fish. Actually, this soup is nice enough on its own – it doesn't even need seafood.

400 g cooked, frozen prawns, shelled
2 tablespoons butter
$^1/_2$ cup cake flour
4 cups milk
1 x 60 g packet white onion soup powder
1 cup water
1 x 25 g packet Ina Paarman's Real Chicken Stock
1 x 415 g can creamed sweet corn
1 x 50 g sachet tomato paste
freshly ground black pepper

Defrost the prawns overnight and drain the liquid. (You can obviously also use fresh prawns, if available, but in that case you have to cook them first. It only takes a few minutes.) Heat the butter, flour and 3 cups of milk in a large pot while whisking continuously. Stir until the mixture thickens. Mix the soup powder and the water together, then stir it into the remaining cup of milk and then add to the soup and stir through. Add the chicken stock and let the mixture simmer for 5 minutes over moderate heat while stirring continuously. Add the sweet corn, tomato paste and prawns and let it simmer until it has warmed through. Dilute the soup with boiling water if it is too thick for your liking. Don't make the soup too long in advance and don't overcook it. Grind some black pepper over and serve immediately.

Butternut and tomato soup

Serves 6

This recipe will surprise your taste buds with its combination of the trusty butternut and tarty tomato. It's practical too, because butternut can last for weeks in the bush.

3 tablespoons olive oil
2 onions, peeled and chopped
3 cups raw cubed butternut
1 x 410 g can whole tomatoes
1 chicken stock cube
1 teaspoon curry powder
4 cups boiling water
1 x 250 ml carton long-life cream (optional)
1 tablespoon dried parsley
salt and pepper to taste

Heat the oil over medium heat in a pot and fry the onions until soft. Add the butternut, tomatoes, chicken stock cube, curry and boiling water. Simmer over low heat until the butternut is soft; this takes 20–30 minutes. Drain the liquid and set aside for later use. Mash the vegetables with a potato masher. Pour the liquid back into the pot and stir it through the vegetables. If you are using cream add it and the parsley now. Taste if the soup is salty enough, and season to taste. Heat the soup on low heat until it's warmed through and grind over some black pepper.

Sweet potato soup

Serves 6

Sweet potatoes keep well on safari and one can prepare them in many ways to boot. This is an appetising, warm and well-flavoured soup.

2 tablespoons cake flour
$1/2$ cup water
4 cups mashed cooked sweet potatoes
2 tablespoons butter
1 teaspoon salt
$1/2$ teaspoon ground cinnamon
1 teaspoon ground ginger
$1/2$ teaspoon ground nutmeg
2 tablespoons honey
2 bay leaves
3–4 cups boiling water, depending on how thick you want the soup to be
1 chicken or vegetable stock cube
1 x 400 g can coconut cream (or coconut milk)
1 x 400 g can chickpeas, drained and rinsed

Mix the flour with the $1/2$ cup water until the lumps have dissolved. Place the flour mixture and the remaining ingredients into a cast-iron pot and heat over low heat. Stir continuously until warm and then serve.

Fish and seafood

Calamari rings
Serves 4

There are few things as enjoyable as the combination of calamari, chips, chilli sauce and lemon wedges...

Batter
$1/2$ cup cake flour
1 teaspoon baking powder
a pinch of salt
1 egg
1 tablespoon olive oil
$1/2$ cup milk or water

Calamari
1 kg raw calamari rings
oil for deep-frying

For the batter: Mix the flour, baking powder and salt together in a bowl. Make a well in the middle of the flour mixture and add the egg, olive oil and milk or water. Whisk until the batter is smooth. Heat the oil until hot – drop a small piece of batter in the oil and if it starts sizzling, the oil is hot enough.

For the calamari: Dip the calamari rings into the batter with a fork and then fry the rings in batches until the batter is golden brown. Don't fry too many rings at once, otherwise they'll go soggy. Spoon the fried calamari rings onto paper towels to drain the oil. Serve with salt, chilli sauce, lemon wedges and potato chips.

Tip: If you're using frozen calamari rings, defrost them properly beforehand and make 100% sure the rings are dry before dipping them in the batter, otherwise the batter won't stick to the calamari.

Trout spread
Makes 2 cups

Trout is among the tastiest freshwater fish. This easy and versatile spread can also be used as a pancake filling.

200 g cooked or smoked trout, skinned and finely
    flaked (see tip)
$1/2$ cup smooth cottage cheese
4 tablespoons mayonnaise
a dash of lemon juice
freshly ground black pepper (you don't need salt if you
    are using smoked trout)

Mix all the ingredients together and serve. The spread is particularly nice served with avocado – spoon tablespoonsful on top of avocado halves as a starter. Or you can serve it on savoury crackers, bread rolls or thin slices of toast.

Tip: 200 g trout equals $1 1/2$ cups finely flaked fish. It is highly unlikely that you will be taking a kitchen scale along on safari.

Fish stew
Serves 6

Catch your own fish or use frozen fish for this mouthwatering fish stew.

2 tablespoons cake flour, mixed with $^1/_4$ teaspoon salt
4 tablespoons turmeric
450 g hake (or any other white fish), cut into large chunks
3 tablespoons oil
1 onion, peeled and chopped
4 sweet potatoes, peeled, cubed and cooked
1 teaspoon ground coriander
2 teaspoons curry powder
$^1/_2$ cup seedless sultanas or raisins, soaked in 1 cup water
1 x 410 g can Indian-style tomatoes (or any other canned tomatoes)
1 x 50 g sachet tomato paste
3 tablespoons soft brown sugar
1 x 175 g tub plain yoghurt
a handful of fresh coriander leaves, chopped or 2 tablespoons dried
   coriander leaves or parsley
1 teaspoon salt

Combine the flour and turmeric. Roll the fish in the flour mixture and coat well. Meanwhile, heat the oil in a pot. Fry the fish until golden brown. Remove the fish and set aside. Put the onion in the same pot and fry until soft. Add the sweet potatoes, ground coriander and curry, and stir for 1 minute. Add the sultanas or raisins (water and all), tomatoes, tomato paste and brown sugar. Stir through and simmer over low heat for about 5 minutes until the mixture thickens slightly. Now return the fish to the pan and simmer until hot. Remove from the heat and stir in the yoghurt and coriander leaves. Serve with a big bowl of rice.

Variation: You can substitute the sweet potatoes with cubes of boiled potato, and you can also replace the yoghurt with coconut milk or coconut cream, if you can afford the calories!

Fish bobotie
Serves 4–6

The ocean is a source of healthy and tasty foods that can be prepared in many exciting ways. Try your hand at this tasty fish bobotie.

1 onion, peeled and chopped
1 tablespoon oil
2 tablespoons chutney
3 tablespoons wine vinegar
2 teaspoons curry powder
1 teaspoon turmeric
1 teaspoon sugar
salt and pepper to taste
1/4 cup boiling water
1 thick slice white bread, crusts removed, soaked in milk

500 g cooked white fish, bones removed, flaked
2 tablespoons sultanas or seedless raisins
3 eggs
4 bay leaves
1/2 cup milk

Fry the onion in the oil until soft. Add the chutney, vinegar, curry powder, turmeric, sugar, salt and pepper. Add the water and stir through until the sauce thickens. Squeeze the milk out of the bread and into a separate bowl and set aside for later use. Mix the bread and fish together. Add the bread mixture and sultanas to the curry sauce. Beat one of the eggs and add to the curry sauce. Place a wire rack into a cast-iron pot. Spoon the fish mixture into a greased, fireproof dish that will fit into the pot. Push the bay leaves halfway into the bobotie. Beat the remaining eggs and milk together to make the egg custard. Pour the custard over the bobotie. Place the bobotie onto the wire rack in the pot and bake for 30 minutes or until the custard has set. Pack hot coals on the lid of the cast-iron pot so the heat comes mainly from the top. Serve with sliced bananas and chutney.

Tip: If you want to give the bobotie a modern twist simply bake it in a bigger container. The layer of bobotie will be thinner and you can use a cookie cutter or a small glass to press out bobotie rounds. Arrange the bobotie rounds on top of each other on the serving plates. Now you have mini-towers of food in the bush!

Snoek on an open fire

Serves 4–6

This recipe has always been a favourite. If you are a bit inexperienced when it comes to making fish on the fire, this recipe is the perfect introduction as it is not only delectable but also very easy.

Marinade
1/2 cup olive oil
1/2 cup smooth apricot jam
2 tablespoons chutney
juice of 1 lemon

1 kg half-smoked or fresh snoek, butterflied

Spray a hinged grid with nonstick cooking spray and set aside for later use. Whisk together all the marinade ingredients in a small pot and heat over medium heat until the jam has melted. Place the fish on the hinged grid and brush the marinade on both sides of the fish. Close the grid and place the fish approximately 30 cm above the coals with its skin side facing the fire. Turn the fish every 2 minutes, brushing marinade over it with every turn. Open the grid with every turn to loosen the fish and to prevent it sticking to the grid. Braai the snoek until it is cooked – test by cutting the thickest piece of meat and if it's not watery it is cooked through. Serve with garlic- or pot bread.

Tip: As the sugar in the apricot jam burns easily, you need to ensure the fish does not burn by turning it constantly. You will be spending most of your time next to the fire to keep an eye on the fish.

Fish balls

Makes 12 meatballs

You can replace the canned fish with fresh, cooked fish, just ensure that all the bones have been removed.

2 slices white bread, crusts removed, soaked in milk
2 x 170 g cans shredded tuna in brine, drained
1 small onion, peeled and grated
1 egg, beaten
2 teaspoons dried parsley
1 teaspoon ginger paste
1/2 teaspoon ground cumin
1/2 teaspoon turmeric
1/2 teaspoon ground coriander
1/4 teaspoon salt
1/2 teaspoon white pepper
oil for frying
1/2 cup cake flour

Squeeze the milk out of the bread and discard. Mix the bread, tuna, onion, egg, parsley, ginger, cumin, turmeric, coriander, salt and pepper together. Shape the mixture into balls and then refrigerate for 30 minutes. Heat the oil over medium heat. Roll the meatballs in the flour and fry until done. Serve with lemon wedges and sweet chilli sauce.

Chicken

Butter chicken
Serves 4

Butter chicken must be one of the most popular curry meals. It is very rich and can be served in small portions.

4 tablespoons butter
1 medium onion, peeled and grated
1 garlic clove, peeled and crushed
1 heaped teaspoon ginger paste
1 x 690 g bottle tomato purée
1 cup water
$^1/_4$ teaspoon sugar
1 teaspoon ground cumin
1 teaspoon ground coriander
1 tablespoon curry powder
$^1/_2$ teaspoon chilli flakes
1 teaspoon salt
$^1/_2$ teaspoon ground black pepper
8 chicken pieces (thighs and drumsticks – skin removed)
4 tablespoons double cream
a handful of cashews, roasted

Melt the butter in a pot. Add the onion, garlic and ginger paste and stir for a minute or two. Add the tomato purée, water, sugar, cumin, coriander, curry powder, chilli flakes, salt and pepper. Add the chicken pieces. Stir through well and arrange the chicken pieces in such a manner that they are covered with sauce. Cover and simmer for about 1 hour on low heat until the chicken is soft. Remove from the heat and stir in the cream. Put the chicken in a deep bowl and sprinkle over the cashews before serving with rice and a salad or vegetables of your choice.

Fragrant chicken stew
Serves 4–6

This chicken stew is not only fast and easy to make but also delicious.

3 tablespoons cooking oil
1 kg chicken portions (thighs and drumsticks – skin removed)
$^1/_2$ cup cake flour
1 garlic clove, peeled and chopped
1 teaspoon chilli flakes
2 potatoes, peeled and cubed
1 x 410 g can tomatoes
1 x 50 g sachet tomato paste
2 cups boiling water
1 x 410 g can whole kernel corn, drained
1 x 410 g can sugar beans, drained
1 green pepper, seeded and diced
salt and pepper to taste

Heat the oil over medium heat. Roll the chicken portions in the flour and then fry until they are golden brown all over. Add the garlic, chilli, potatoes, tomatoes, tomato paste and boiling water to the chicken. Simmer over moderate heat for 1 hour. Add the corn, sugar beans, green pepper and season to taste. Simmer for 15 minutes. Serve on rice or with naan bread.

Chicken and lentil curry

Serves 6

Chicken has always been a lifesaver, especially when the economic strings are a bit tighter. Add some veggies and lentils to the chicken and you can almost feed a whole army of people.

2 tablespoons oil
1 onion, peeled and chopped
1 garlic clove, peeled and crushed
2 tablespoons curry powder
4 deboned and skinless chicken breasts, cubed
2 cups chicken stock
2 tomatoes, peeled and diced
2 heaped tablespoons desiccated coconut flakes
1 tablespoon vinegar
1 green apple, peeled, cored and cubed
2 potatoes, peeled and cubed
1 cup red lentils
1 cup chopped green beans
1 cup peeled and cubed butternut
1 teaspoon salt
1 x 175 g tub plain yoghurt (or 1 x 165 ml can coconut milk)

Heat the oil in a pot and fry the onion and garlic until soft. Add the curry powder and stir through. Add the chicken and stir for about a minute to combine. Add all the remaining ingredients, except the yoghurt, and turn down the heat. Allow the mixture to simmer, covered, for 30 minutes, until the lentils and vegetables are soft. Stir often to avoid the lentils burning. If the mixture is a bit dry add boiling water until you reach the desired consistency. When the vegetables and lentils are soft, remove the pot from the heat and stir in the yoghurt. Serve with rice.

Hawaiian chicken pizzas

Serves 6

Who doesn't like pizza?

12 thick slices white bread or pot bread
butter for spreading on the bread
1 cup sliced onion
1 cup grated tomato or 1 x 410 g can whole Italian-style tomatoes, chopped
salt and pepper to taste
2 cups leftover chicken, cut into strips
1 x 440 g can pineapple pieces, well drained and chopped
2 cups grated Cheddar or mozzarella cheese

Press out a circle from each slice of bread with a large cup or glass. Toast the bread circles on both sides by placing them over hot coals for a few minutes. Watch the bread closely, as you don't want to burn it. Spread butter on one side of each bread circle. Divide the sliced onion and tomato between the bread circles and place on top of the buttered side. Season to taste and arrange the chicken and pineapple on top. Sprinkle the cheese over. Make a few pizzas at a time by placing the pizza rounds on a sheet of heavy-duty foil on a braai grid over hot coals. After the cheese has melted, remove the pizza rounds with an egg lifter to prevent the pizzas from breaking.

Chicken meatballs

Makes 15 meatballs

This recipe is ideal for leftover chicken breasts. If you're packing it as padkos, keep it in the cool box – chicken is not to be trifled with, especially if it's travelling far.

2 slices white bread, crusts removed, soaked in milk
4 chicken breasts, cooked, deboned, skin removed, shredded
1 small onion, peeled and grated
1 egg, beaten
2 teaspoons grated lemon zest
$^1/_2$ green pepper, seeded and finely sliced
$^1/_4$ teaspoon chilli flakes
2 teaspoons dried parsley
1 teaspoon salt
$^1/_4$ teaspoon white pepper
$^1/_2$ cup cake flour
oil for frying

Squeeze the milk out of the bread and discard. Mix the bread and the rest of the ingredients, except the cake flour and oil, together. Shape the mixture into small balls between your hands and squeeze them hard to make sturdy meatballs. Heat the oil over medium heat. Roll the meatballs in the flour and cook in moderately-hot oil. As is the case with any meatball, chicken meat balls can taste a bit dry as a main course. No one will complain if you serve them with cheese, sweet chilli or any other sauce, and sweet potatoes. For *padkos*, however, they're delicious on their own or with a sandwich and boiled egg.

Chicken livers

Serves 4

Chicken livers with a bite are always a hit. The amount of chilli in this recipe is for decent people who believe in moderation, but you can always add more or even leave it out altogether.

3 tablespoons oil
1 large onion, peeled and finely chopped
2 x 250 g containers chicken livers, rinsed and dried
2 ripe tomatoes, peeled and finely chopped
$^1/_2$ teaspoon chilli flakes
salt and pepper to taste

Heat the oil in a pot and fry the onion until soft. Add the chicken livers and fry until they are brown and cooked through. Stir in the tomatoes and the rest of the ingredients and simmer for a few minutes until the sauce is nice and thick. Serve with toast, cut into triangles, or soft bread rolls. Add a little Mrs Ball's chilli chutney for fun.

Variation: If you prefer to save your fresh tomatoes for another recipe, replace them with a can of chopped tomatoes or a sachet of tomato paste.

Cola chicken

Serves 4

This old stalwart is still a popular safari recipe.

2 tablespoons butter or oil
8 chicken breasts, deboned and skin removed
  if preferred
2 cups Coca-Cola® (not Light or Zero – the sugar
  content is vital for a syrupy sauce)
1 tablespoon golden syrup
1 tablespoon soy sauce
$^1/_2$ teaspoon salt
$^1/_2$ teaspoon white pepper

Heat the oil or butter in a pot over medium heat and lightly fry the chicken until golden brown. Add the Coca-Cola®, cover and simmer for 45 minutes or until the chicken is cooked and tender. Add the remaining ingredients and boil uncovered until the sauce turns brown and sticky. Serve with mash and a green salad.

Chicken *potjie*

Serves 4

If you are planning a safari menu you should include at least one potjie recipe. This recipe is easy enough to try for those who are inexperienced potjie chefs.

2 tablespoons oil
2 onions, peeled and chopped
1 whole chicken, cut into portions (or legs and thighs),
  deboned and skin removed if preferred
2 cups boiling water
5 sweet potatoes, peeled and thickly sliced
5 carrots, peeled and thickly sliced
2 potatoes, peeled and thickly sliced
1 cup dry white wine
2 teaspoons soy sauce
1 x 50 g sachet tomato paste
2 tablespoons brown sugar
salt and pepper to taste

Heat the oil in a *potjie* and fry the onions until soft. Add the chicken and fry until brown. Add 1 cup of the water and stir through to ensure there's liquid at the bottom of the *potjie*. Pack the vegetables on top of the chicken. In a separate bowl, mix the remaining water, white wine, soy sauce, tomato paste, sugar and seasoning together, and pour over the vegetables. Cover and let the *potjie* simmer for 1–2 hours over low heat until all the ingredients are soft and fragrant. Check the potjie often to make sure that it doesn't dry out and add a little water if necessary. The experts say you shouldn't stir a *potjie* at all, but who likes being told what to do?

Paella
Serves 4

Paella is a great way to use up leftover rice and contains a mixture of seafood, chicken and other meat. You get dozens of variations and can adapt it to taste. For instance, you might not get nice, fresh prawns for sale in Botswana, but in Mozambique they're practically a staple.

2 tablespoons oil
1 onion, peeled and chopped
2 chicken breasts, cooked and sliced
1 x 225 g chorizo sausage, sliced (you can replace it with salami)
4 rashers bacon, fried and cut into small pieces
1 red pepper, seeded and sliced
1 x 50 g sachet tomato paste
2 teaspoons paprika
1 garlic clove, peeled and finely chopped
12 prawns, cooked and shelled, tails intact
1 chicken stock cube, dissolved in 1 cup boiling water
1 cup frozen peas
$^1/_2$ teaspoon chilli flakes
juice of 1 lime or lemon
2 cups cooked rice
freshly ground black pepper

Heat the oil in a pan over moderate heat and fry the onion until soft. Add the rest of the ingredients, except the rice and black pepper, and simmer for 5 minutes. Add the rice, mix through until hot, sprinkle black pepper over and serve with a glass of ice-cold dry white wine.

Tip: Paella is already salty enough and you do not need to add more salt. People who want more salt can add some afterwards.

Peri-peri butterfly chicken

Serves 4

It's not that difficult to braai a chicken – you must just be sure the coals aren't too hot. Over too high heat, the skin will burn while the meat will still be raw inside. If you're still worried, rather use chicken pieces – they braai faster than a whole chicken.

Chicken
3 tablespoons butter
1 tablespoon chilli flakes
juice of 1 lemon
2 garlic cloves, peeled and
   crushed
1 teaspoon paprika
2 teaspoons olive oil
1 teaspoon salt
1.5 kg butterflied chicken

Sauce
2 tablespoons butter
2 tablespoons olive oil
2 garlic cloves, peeled and
   crushed
1 teaspoon chilli flakes
juice of $^{1}/_{2}$ lemon
1 teaspoon dried parsley

For the chicken: Mix the butter, chilli flakes, lemon juice, garlic, paprika, olive oil and salt. Rub the mixture over both sides of the chicken and let it marinate for 1 hour (or overnight if possible) in the fridge. Braai until the chicken is done through. It usually takes $1^{1}/_{2}$ hours to cook all the way through. Make sure the grid is fairly high above the coals, otherwise the chicken will burn long before it's done.

For the sauce: Melt the butter in a small saucepan and add the olive oil and garlic. Sauté for 2 minutes over low heat. Ensure that the garlic doesn't burn. Remove the garlic from the oil with a spoon and discard. Add the rest of the ingredients. Drizzle the sauce over the chicken as soon as it's done, or serve it in a bowl so everyone can help themselves.

Chicken with tequila and cinnamon

Serves 4–6

If your chick's marinated overnight, you're a mere 15 minutes away from serving a meal that is a welcome variation on the usual chicken recipe.

8 chicken breasts, deboned and skin removed
$^1\!/_2$ cup good tequila
juice of 1 fresh lemon
1 garlic clove, peeled and chopped
1 tablespoon brown sugar
1 large cinnamon stick
1 tablespoon butter
4 tablespoons olive oil
1 chicken stock cube, dissolved in 1 cup boiling water
$^1\!/_2$ teaspoon ground cinnamon
2 whole cloves
$^1\!/_2$ teaspoon ground black pepper
$^1\!/_2$ teaspoon chilli flakes
1 x 250 ml container long-life cream
salt to taste, but the chicken stock is probably salty enough

Put the chicken breasts in a large Ziploc® bag. Mix the tequila, lemon juice, garlic and brown sugar together in a small bowl, then pour the mixture over the chicken and add the cinnamon stick to the marinade. Seal the bag and marinate the chicken for 1–2 hours (or overnight if possible), in the camping fridge. Just before the meal and after you've knocked together a salad, heat the butter and olive oil in a pot. Brown the chicken on both sides. Remove the cinnamon stick from the marinade and keep it for later use. Add the stock and marinade and simmer for about 10 minutes. Add the cinnamon stick, ground cinnamon, cloves, black pepper and chilli to the pot and stir for 5 minutes over low heat to release the spices' flavours. Add the cream and stir it in until it's warm. Immediately remove the pot from the heat so that the cream doesn't curdle. Remove the chicken from the pot and place onto plates. Drizzle over the sauce and if the breasts still look a little bland, sprinkle over some paprika or cayenne pepper. Garnish with some extra cinnamon sticks if you prefer.

Meaty mains

Oxtail stew
Serves 4

This stew is mouthwateringly delicious when it has simmered for 5 to 6 hours. Of course you have to keep the fire going for this long, but it is well worthwhile.

2 tablespoons oil
1 kg oxtail
$^1/_2$ cup cake flour
2 onions, peeled and chopped
2 carrots, peeled and cut into thick rounds
2 celery sticks, chopped
1 cup good quality red wine
1 x 500 ml container organic beef stock (or dissolve
   1 beef stock cube in 2 cups boiling water)
1 x 410 g can tomatoes
1 x 50 g sachet tomato paste
$1^1/_2$ tablespoons orange marmalade

Heat the oil in a pot. Roll the oxtail in the flour and then fry, sealing all the sides. When the oxtail has been fried on all its sides, add the onions and fry for a few more minutes. Add the carrots and celery and fry for a few minutes. Add the red wine and let the mixture boil while you add the remaining ingredients and stir through. Place a tight-fitting lid on the pot. Ensure that the stew simmers slowly over low heat for 5–6 hours. Every once in a while, you can check that there is still enough liquid and that the meat hasn't started catching, but the liquid should last until the end of the cooking process. It is unlikely that you'll have to add more salt as the beef stock usually contains enough salt, but have a taste and add more if needed.

Beef Madras
Serves 4

Traditionally this is a hot curry, but you can omit the chilli – it will still be tasty.

2 tablespoons butter
2 onions, peeled and chopped
2 garlic cloves, peeled and crushed
1 teaspoon ginger paste
1 teaspoon chilli flakes
2 teaspoons ground coriander
2 teaspoons ground turmeric
$^1/_4$ teaspoon white pepper
1 kg deboned, cubed beef
1 cup boiling water
1 x 400 g can coconut cream
1 teaspoon salt
juice of $^1/_4$ lemon
desiccated coconut to sprinkle on top

Melt the butter in a pot and fry the onions and garlic until soft. Add the ginger paste, chilli flakes, coriander, turmeric and pepper and stir for a few seconds to combine. Add the meat and stir for another minute or two until the meat is covered in the spices. Add the water and coconut cream. Cover the pot and simmer on low heat for $1^1/_2$ hours or until the meat is tender. Check often that there is enough liquid and add water if necessary. If the mixture is too watery at the end of the cooking process, boil it uncovered over high heat to reduce and thicken the sauce. Lastly, stir in the salt and lemon juice. Sprinkle desiccated coconut over each serving.

Silverside and potatoes

Serves 4–6

This tasty piece of beef takes a long time to cook and it is perfect for those days when you plan to spend the whole day in the camp – you can simply check every 30 minutes that there's still enough water in the pot.

3 tablespoons oil
1 kg beef silverside
2 onions, peeled and chopped
2 tomatoes, peeled and finely chopped
$1/2$ bottle good red wine
boiling water
salt and pepper to taste
6 potatoes, peeled and quartered

Heat the oil in a flat-bottomed cast-iron pot and brown the meat. Remove the meat from the pot and set aside. Add the onions to the pot and cook until they are golden brown, and then add the tomatoes. Stir for a few minutes until the tomatoes are soft. Put the meat back into the pot, add the wine and enough boiling water to just cover the meat. Place the lid on the pot and cook over low heat for $2^1/2$–3 hours. Check the liquid level often and do not let it boil dry. Remove the lid for the last hour to let the sauce reduce and thicken. Season to taste. About 30 minutes before you take the pot off the coals, add the potatoes and cook slowly in the tasty gravy.

Chakalaka cottage pie

Serves 6

It is always fun to take a recipe and add some African flavour to it. That's exactly what you are doing by adding a can of chakalaka to this recipe. You can use any chakalaka your family likes. The chakalaka used in this recipe has sweet corn in it and not that much chilli – it's perfect if you're catering for children too.

1 tablespoon oil
1 onion, peeled and chopped
500 g beef mince
1 x 50 g sachet tomato paste
1 x 410 g can chakalaka with sweet corn
1 cup frozen peas
water
salt and pepper to taste
3 large sweet potatoes, peeled and cubed
1 tablespoon butter
$\pm^1/2$ cup milk

Heat the oil in a pot and fry the onion until soft. Add the mince and fry until browned. Add the tomato paste, chakalaka, peas and a little water and simmer for a few minutes. Season to taste. Boil the sweet potatoes in salted water until cooked, then drain and mash with a potato masher or a fork. Season to taste, then add the butter and enough milk to form a smooth mixture. Spoon the mince into a dish and top with the sweet potato mash. Eat as is if you are cooking in the bush. At home you can bake it in the oven for 30 minutes. This will brown the sweet potato layer nicely.

Sticky ribs

Serves 4

The "sticky" in the recipe title does not refer to the tender meat but rather to the rib sauce that sticks to your fingers. The secret to making tender ribs is to cook the meat beforehand to ensure it's as soft as can be.

1 onion, peeled and quartered
3 cups water
1 beef stock cube, dissolved in ¼ cup boiling water
1 kg pork or lamb ribs, cut into pieces of 1–2 ribs each
1 x 500 ml bottle Wellington sticky spare rib marinade

Place the onion pieces in a large pan and add the water, stock and ribs. Simmer slowly until soft (about 1½ hours). Remove the ribs, place in a bowl and discard the liquid and onion. Add half of the marinade to the ribs and let it marinate in the fridge for at least 2 hours. Wipe most of the marinade off the meat with a paper towel and brush the rest of the marinade over the meat while you are braaiing. Braai over moderate coals for 10 minutes, depending on how thick the ribs have been cut. The temperature of the coals is important, as the meat will burn due to the sugar in the marinade if the coals are too hot.

Chilli con carne

Serves 6

Mince and baked beans make for an appetising and hearty filling for the ravenous 4 x 4 cowboys. Eat it on toast, baked potatoes or as a pancake filling.

2 tablespoons oil
1 onion, peeled and finely chopped
2 garlic cloves, peeled and finely chopped
500 g lean beef mince
1 carrot, peeled and finely diced
1 teaspoon salt
1 teaspoon ground coriander
1 teaspoon cumin
1 teaspoon chilli flakes
1 x 400 g can chopped tomatoes
1 x 50 g sachet tomato paste
1 small green pepper, seeded and finely diced
1 x 410 g can baked beans in tomato sauce

Heat the oil in a pan and fry the onion and garlic until soft. Add the mince and fry the meat until it's broken up and brown. Add the carrot, salt, coriander, cumin, chilli, tomatoes and tomato paste and let the mixture simmer for about 15 minutes, or until the carrot is soft. Mix in the green pepper and beans and stir until heated through before serving.

Tip: Sour cream goes well with this filling – if you can get your hands on it in the bush.

Greek leg of lamb
Serves 8

You can serve this leg of lamb without the sauce if you wish, but once you have tasted this finger-licking delight, you will never again serve lamb without it.

Lamb
$^1/_4$ cup olive oil
$^1/_4$ cup freshly squeezed lemon
   juice
1 teaspoon dried rosemary
1 garlic clove, bruised (if you love
   garlic, add more)
1.5 kg deboned leg of lamb,
   butterflied
salt and pepper to taste

Yoghurt sauce
2 tablespoons butter
4 tablespoons cake flour
1 x 150 ml tub plain yoghurt
2 cups buttermilk
1 teaspoon dried parsley
2 teaspoons dried chives
$^1/_4$ teaspoon salt
$^1/_4$ teaspoon pepper

For the lamb: Mix the olive oil, lemon juice, rosemary and garlic together in an airtight plastic container. Place the leg of lamb into the container, seal and marinate overnight in the camping fridge. Braai the meat on a grid over low heat for 2 hours or until cooked to your taste. Sprinkle salt and pepper over the leg of lamb and serve with the yoghurt sauce.

For the yoghurt sauce: Melt the butter in a saucepan over low heat and rapidly stir in the flour until the lumps have dissolved. Add the remaining ingredients. Allow to simmer over low heat for a minute or two (the yoghurt will curdle if the heat is too high). Serve the yoghurt sauce and warm meat together.

Tip: If your trip to the bundu is too long to consider packing in fresh buttermilk you can replace it with 1 cup long-life cream and 1 cup long-life milk.

Curry meatballs

Makes 30 meatballs

Don't be put off by the long list of ingredients – it's not that complicated, and once you've tasted the meatballs you will understand why all these ingredients are vital in making the yummiest meatballs ever.

Meatballs
1 kg beef mince
1 large onion, peeled and grated
1 cup raw oats
$^1/_2$ cup tomato sauce
3 tablespoons Worcestershire sauce
2 tablespoons chutney
2 tablespoons apricot jam
$^1/_2$ cup white wine
1 tablespoon ground coriander
$^1/_2$ teaspoon ground cloves
2 eggs, beaten
2 teaspoons salt
$^1/_2$ teaspoon white pepper

1 cup cake flour
$^1/_2$ cup boiling water

Curry sauce
1 large onion, peeled, finely
    chopped and fried in oil
    until soft
1 teaspoon ground cloves
1 cup white wine vinegar
$^1/_2$ cup chutney
3 tablespoons apricot jam
3 tablespoons curry powder
$^1/_4$ teaspoon salt

For the meatballs: Mix all the ingredients for the meatballs, except the cake flour and water, together. Shape into meatballs and roll them in the flour. Heat a little oil in a pan over moderate heat. If the oil is too hot, the meatballs will burn before they're done. Fry on one side until the meatballs are firm and then carefully turn them over with a spoon. Brown the other side and test whether they're done by breaking one of the meatballs open. If you are making these at home, preheat the oven to 180 °C. Place the meatballs in an ovenproof dish, pour the water into the dish and bake for 15–20 minutes or until they are cooked (the baking time depends on the size of the meatballs). Break one of the meatballs open to test if it is done.

For the curry sauce: Mix all the sauce ingredients together and simmer over low heat for 15 minutes while stirring continuously. Pour the hot sauce over the meatballs and serve.

Italian meatballs

Makes 15 meatballs

Prepare these meatballs at home and take them along on safari in the freezer. Keep the meatballs and sauce in separate containers.

Meatballs
oil for frying
3 pork bangers, skin removed
1 cup beef mince
$1/2$ small onion, peeled and finely chopped
1 garlic clove, peeled and crushed
2 slices white bread, crusts removed, soaked in milk
1 egg, beaten
2 teaspoons dried parsley
$1/2$ teaspoon salt
$1/4$ teaspoon white pepper

Tomato sauce
2 tablespoons oil
1 large onion, peeled and grated
1 garlic clove, peeled and crushed
$1/2$ cup dry white wine
1 x 690 g bottle Italian tomato purée
$1/2$ teaspoon salt
freshly ground black pepper

For the meatballs: Heat the oil in a pan until moderately hot. Squeeze the milk out of the bread and discard. While the oil is heating, mix all the meatball ingredients together. Shape the mixture between two tablespoons and place in the oil. The mixture will be quite soft. Fry until done.

For the sauce: Heat the oil in a pan. Fry the onion and garlic for a few minutes. Add the wine and tomato purée and season to taste. Simmer for 15 minutes and pour over the cooked meatballs. Serve with spaghetti and some grated Parmesan.

Easy ostrich burgers

Makes 6 patties

The nice thing about making these tasty burgers is that they are ridiculously easy to make and, best of all, they won't send your cholesterol levels rocketing.

500 g ostrich mince
1 large onion, peeled and grated
2 thick slices bread, crusts removed, soaked in
   $^1/_2$ cup milk
1 teaspoon salt
$^1/_2$ teaspoon white pepper
oil for frying

Mix the mince and onion together. Squeeze the milk out of the bread, discard the milk and crumble the bread into mince mixture. Mix in the salt and pepper. Shape six hamburger patties, flatten them slightly with your hand and refrigerate for 1–2 hours. Heat the oil in a pan and fry the patties until nicely browned and done. Serve in bread rolls with a slice of tomato, onion, lettuce and a tasty sauce.

Tip: Try bottled burger sauces, such as onion marmalade and cranberry sauce with these ostrich burgers. It adds extra zip to an already tasty meal.

Lamb kleftiko

Serves 4

This meal is easy to prepare and delectable, but it has to be cooked for as long as possible over low to medium heat. Therefore, light the fire early afternoon and put the lamb on the coals to cook until soft as marrow.

4 lamb shanks
heavy-duty foil (enough for 4 double-layered
   large parcels)
4 handfuls chopped vegetables (e.g. potatoes, pumpkin,
   onions and sweet peppers)
1 x 240 g can artichokes, drained (optional)
4 tablespoons olive oil
juice of 1 lemon
1 teaspoon grated lemon zest
4 garlic cloves, peeled and chopped
$^1/_4$ cup dry white wine
1 teaspoon dried rosemary
1 teaspoon dried thyme
2 teaspoons salt
1 teaspoon ground black pepper

Place the lamb shanks on the double-layered foil, arrange the vegetables around the meat, sprinkle the remaining ingredients over each packet and fold up the foil securely. Place the parcels on a grid over low to medium-hot coals and turn them over every 30 minutes. Cook for 2 hours, but if you can stretch it to 3–4 hours you will be rewarded with meat that simply falls off the bone. Remove the outer layer of foil and serve individual packets of kleftiko.

Hint: If you prefer your vegetables crisp you can add them to the foil parcels later in the cooking process.

Cape Malay bean stew
Serves 4

Who would have thought that green beans can taste so good when served in a stew?

1 large onion, peeled and chopped
1 garlic clove, peeled and chopped
2 tablespoons oil
500 g lamb cubed
boiling water
$^1/_2$ teaspoon chilli flakes
$2^1/_2$ cups washed, topped and tailed, and chopped
   green beans
2 potatoes, peeled and cubed
1 teaspoon salt
$^1/_2$ teaspoon white pepper
1 teaspoon sugar

Fry the onion and garlic in oil in a pot until the onion is soft. Add the meat and fry until brown. Cover the meat with boiling water and simmer for $1^1/_2$ hours. Add the remaining ingredients and simmer for another hour until the meat is nice and soft. If the stew looks too watery by the end of the cooking process, cook it on high heat uncovered, for a short while to reduce the liquid.

Granny's *sosaties* (kebabs)
Makes 12–15 kebabs

Making sosaties on safari is not that difficult, but you have to remember to start marinating the meat about two days before the braai takes place. Because the meat cubes are smaller than a whole leg, they braai much faster.

2 large onions, peeled and quartered
1 tablespoon curry powder
1 teaspoon turmeric
1 cup white wine vinegar
1 cup medium-sweet sherry or white wine
$^1/_2$ cup fruit chutney
4 lemon leaves
1 lemon, cut into segments
salt and pepper to taste
1 kg deboned leg of lamb, cut into 2.5-cm cubes
kebab skewers

Simmer the onions in a little water for 5 minutes in a saucepan. Add the curry powder, turmeric, vinegar, sherry or white wine, chutney, lemon leaves, lemon segments and seasoning. Cook for a few minutes. Let it cool slightly and then pour the marinade over the meat cubes. Marinate in a sealed plastic container in the camping fridge for two days while turning the meat now and again. Soak the skewers in water for 1 hour to prevent them from burning. Thread the meat and onions alternately onto the skewers. Braai over medium-hot coals until done.

Variation: You can also add green pepper and/or dried apricots to the marinade and thread them onto the skewers.

Portuguese espetadas

Serves 6

An espetada is the easiest way to quickly prepare a fragrant steak. It's a good idea to invest in a few steel skewers for this purpose. Once you've tasted meat prepared this way, you won't want to braai any other way.

3 garlic cloves, peeled and crushed
2 teaspoons coarse salt
2 teaspoons ground black pepper
3 bay leaves, crushed
juice of 1/2 lemon
1 kg rump steak, cut into 4–5-cm cubes
enough melted butter to brush espetadas

Mix the garlic, salt, pepper, bay leaves and lemon juice together and then add the meat. Rub the mixture into the meat with your hands until it is completely covered. Cover and refrigerate for 1 or 2 hours. Thread the meat onto the stainless steel skewers and brush with the melted butter. Braai over hot coals until the meat cubes are done to your liking.

Tip: It's not a train smash if you don't have espetada steel skewers; you can use standard wooden kebab skewers. Just remember to soak the skewers in water for 1 hour before you start braaiing so that they don't catch alight on the braai.

Pumpkin stew

Serves 4

Pumpkin keeps nice and long in the bundu, which makes it one of the best vegetables for taking along on a trip. It's also frequently on sale at farm stalls. If flat white pumpkins aren't available you can use any other type of pumpkin.

2 tablespoons oil
2 large onions, peeled and chopped
1 kg stewing beef, cubed
3 cinnamon sticks
1 teaspoon chilli flakes
1 teaspoon sugar
1 teaspoon salt
1/2 teaspoon fine white pepper
2-cm piece fresh ginger, peeled and finely chopped (or
    1 teaspoon ground ginger)
boiling water
1 kg flat white pumpkin, peeled and cubed

Heat the oil in a pot and fry the onions until soft. Add the meat and fry until browned. Add the cinnamon, chilli, sugar, salt, white pepper and ginger and stir through. Cover the meat with boiling water. Add the pumpkin and cover. Turn the heat down and let the mixture simmer for about 3 hours. Don't stir the pot – it will cause the pumpkin to disintegrate into an unrecognisable mush. Serve with rice or potatoes.

Rogan josh lamb curry
Serves 4

If you don't like spicy food, simply use less or even no chillies – it will not affect this flavourful meal in the least.

$^1/_2$ cup oil

900 g deboned leg of lamb, cubed

10 green cardamom seeds

2 bay leaves

6 whole cloves

10 black peppercorns

1 cinnamon stick

2 onions, peeled and finely chopped

2 teaspoons ginger paste

2 garlic cloves, peeled and crushed

1 teaspoon ground coriander

1 teaspoon ground cumin

4 teaspoons paprika

1 teaspoon chilli flakes

$1^1/_4$ teaspoon salt

6 tablespoons plain yoghurt

2 cups water

Heat the oil in a saucepan and brown the lamb. As soon as it's all browned, remove and set aside. Add the cardamom seeds, bay leaves, cloves, pepper and cinnamon stick to the same pot. Wait for the cardamom seeds to swell (it takes a few seconds) before adding the onions. Stir for a few minutes until the onions are golden brown. Stir in the ginger paste and garlic. Now add the coriander, cumin, paprika, chilli flakes and salt. Add 1 tablespoon of yoghurt. Stir for 30 seconds and add 1 teaspoon of yoghurt every 30 seconds while stirring continuously on low heat. Now add the water and lamb to the mixture. Stir everything well, cover and simmer on low heat for 2 hours, or until the meat is nice and tender. Check on the curry and stir every 15 minutes so it doesn't catch or burn, and add a little more water if necessary. Remove the lid as soon as the meat is tender. If the sauce isn't thick yet, simmer a little longer until it has reduced and thickened. Remember to remove the cinnamon stick and cardamom seeds before serving.

Tip: The yoghurt takes a while to "get used to" the heat, hence it has to be added bit by bit to stop it from curdling.

Leg of lamb in a pot

Serves 8

The secret behind perfecting this meal is to cook it slowly over low heat.

1.5 kg deboned, rolled leg of lamb
3/4 cup finely chopped dates
10–12 raw (unsalted) cashew nuts, whole or chopped
4 tablespoons oil
2 cups boiling water
1 x 250 ml container long-life cream
2 tablespoons chilli chutney (optional)
salt and pepper to taste

Use a sharp knife to cut about ten 1-cm-deep holes in the leg of lamb and stuff dates and nuts into the holes. Keep some dates for later use. Heat the oil in a flat-bottomed pot over moderately hot coals. As soon as the oil is hot, fry the leg quickly on both sides to seal the meat. Add the boiling water and cover. Cook for about 3 hours over low heat while turning frequently to ensure it doesn't burn (check every now and again that there is enough water in the pot). At the end of the cooking time, just before the leg is cooked, remove the lid to allow the meat juices to thicken. You can check whether the leg has cooked to your taste by making a deep incision in the thickest part of the meat. If the juices are clear, the meat is cooked. While the leg is cooking, simmer the remaining dates, cream and chilli chutney in a saucepan for 10 minutes until the dates are soft, but not pulpy. Remove the lamb from the pot, stir the cream sauce into the meat juices and ensure that it stays hot. Thinly slice the leg of lamb, season to taste and serve with the hot sauce.

Tip: You can add potato cubes to the pot about 30 minutes before the meat is cooked – that way you'll also have a tasty side dish.

Sweet-and-sour pork stew

Serves 4–6

Pork fillet is a tasty cut that is tender if not overcooked. Within an hour you can have a delicious hot stew with a piquant sweet-and-sour sauce.

2 tablespoons oil
2 onions, peeled and chopped
2 garlic cloves, peeled and chopped
1 kg pork fillet, sliced or cubed
1 cup boiling water
1 x 440 g can pineapple pieces (use the fruit and the juice)
1 red sweet pepper, seeded and finely chopped
1 x 250 g punnet button mushrooms, wiped and sliced
1 cup pitted prunes, sliced lengthways into pieces
1 x 50 g sachet tomato paste
2 tablespoons soy sauce
1 teaspoon ground ginger
1 teaspoon salt
1 teaspoon white pepper
2 tablespoons cake flour, mixed with 1/2 cup water (only if needed)

Heat the oil and fry the onions until transluscent. Add the garlic and meat and fry lightly. Add the rest of the ingredients, (except the cake flour and water), and cook for 1 hour or until the meat is soft. If the sauce is too watery at the end of the cooking process, slowly stir in the cake flour mixture and let it simmer for a few minutes until you are satisfied with the thickness of the sauce.

Sweet-and-sour *boerewors*

Serves 6

Ordinary boerie in a hinged braai grid remains a stalwart, but sometimes you'd like a change and that's when you should try this recipe.

1 x 440 g can pineapple rings, drained (keep juice)
1 kg sausage (any sausage will work, but *sosatie* sausage is the nicest)
6 kebab skewers soaked in water
12 cherry tomatoes
12 mild Peppadews®
1 teaspoon mustard powder
1 tablespoon sugar
1 tablespoon lemon juice
1 tablespoon soy sauce

Quarter the pineapple rings. Divide the sausage into six equal pieces and thread each one in the form of a continuous 'S' on its own kebab skewer. Add a piece of pineapple, a cherry tomato and Peppadew® in between each loop of the sausage. Mix the pineapple juice, mustard powder, sugar, lemon juice and soy sauce together. Brush the sauce over the sausage while braaiing it over mild coals. The coals shouldn't be too hot, otherwise the veggies will burn.

Tip: If there is any pineapple left over, you could use it in a mixed salad or carrot salad.

Steak stir-fry

Serves 6

A stir-fry is fast and easy to make – this meal is perfect after a long day on the road when you do not have the energy for hours of cooking.

$1/4$ cup oil
1 onion, peeled and thinly sliced
3 garlic cloves, peeled and crushed
2 cups roughly chopped mixed vegetables (butternut, courgettes, patty pans, and cabbage)
3 cups leftover braaied steak, cut into strips
$1/2$ cup peri-peri cashews (optional)
1 tablespoon brown sugar
1 teaspoon chilli flakes
1 teaspoon ground ginger
1 teaspoon paprika
salt and pepper to taste

Heat the oil in a pan (or a cast-iron flat-bottomed pot) and fry the onion and garlic until golden brown. Add the vegetables and stir-fry until slightly soft. Do not over-cook. Lastly, add the steak and remaining ingredients. Stir until hot and serve on a bed of rice.

Tip: Pour some vinegar into small bowls and place them on the serving table to keep flies at bay.

Kebab tortillas

Serves 6

Try this easy recipe with leftover kebabs.

1 cucumber, cut into strips
3 x 100 ml tubs plain yoghurt or any bottled sauce such as sweet chilli sauce (depending on if you like plain or strong flavours)
2 cups shredded lettuce and cherry tomatoes
salt and pepper to taste
6 tortillas
6 leftover kebabs, skewers removed and the meat quickly warmed in a pan. If vegetables have been skewered in between the meat, heat them too.

Mix the cucumber, yoghurt, lettuce, tomatoes and salt and pepper together. Heat each tortilla separately in a nonstick pan or flat-bottomed pot without oil. It heats up within seconds so don't leave it too long. Wrap the tortillas in a clean dishcloth to keep them warm. When all the tortillas are hot, place the meat cubes in them, add a big spoonful of the cucumber mixture and fold it up so the tortilla resembles an ice-cream cone. Wrapping a serviette around the bottom of the tortilla will hold it together and will prevent the sauce from leaking.

Moroccan mince

Serves 6

You can give mince an exotic flavour by adding interesting spices. Serve with vetkoek, pita bread or couscous.

1-cm piece fresh ginger, peeled
1 garlic clove, peeled
¼ onion, peeled
a few black peppercorns
2 teaspoons ground coriander
2 whole cloves
3 tablespoons oil
500 g beef mince
1 tablespoon mustard seeds
2 potatoes, peeled and cubed
2 teaspoons ground cumin
2 teaspoons curry powder
1 star anise
2 cinnamon sticks
2 cardamom seeds
2 curry leaves
1 teaspoon chilli flakes
1 teaspoon turmeric
1 cup seedless raisins
1 teaspoon salt

Grate the ginger, garlic and onion. Grind the peppercorns, coriander and cloves with a pestle and mortar until fine. Heat the oil and add the ginger mixture and the spice mixture. Fry for 2–3 minutes. Add the mince and fry while stirring continuously to separate the meat. As soon as the mince is brown add the remaining ingredients. Cover with water and simmer covered over low heat for 1 hour.

Tomato stew
Serves 4–6

Most people want a tomato stew like Mom or Granny used to make it. Some believe in using lamb neck, while others use mutton rib or cubed, deboned leg of lamb. Fact is, any cut will do. The meat should have a little bit of fat, but it shouldn't be too fatty.

2 tablespoons oil
3 onions, peeled and chopped
3 garlic cloves, peeled and chopped
1 kg mutton ribs, ribs cut off and halved
6 large, ripe tomatoes, peeled and roughly cut into smaller pieces
1 x 50 g sachet tomato paste
2 teaspoons salt
2 teaspoons sugar
2 teaspoons paprika
3 potatoes, peeled and quartered
1 or 2 tablespoons cake flour, mixed with ½ cup water (if needed)

Heat the oil and fry the onions until soft. Add the garlic and meat and fry until brown. Add the tomatoes, tomato paste, salt, sugar and paprika and stir until mixed. Simmer the stew over moderate heat for 1 hour. It's usually not necessary to add water to the stew, because the tomatoes contain enough liquid, but watch the stew to ensure it has enough liquid. Add the potatoes and cook for another hour or until the ribs are so soft the meat separates from the bone. If the stew is too watery at the end of the cooking process, add the flour and water mixture little by little. Simmer until you are satisfied with the thickness of the sauce. Serve on basmati rice.

Hint: To peel tomatoes, cut a small cross on top of each tomato with a sharp knife. Leave the tomatoes in boiling water for 5 minutes. Pour off the water and pull or rub the peels off – they will come off easily.

Meat pie in a braai grid

Serves 4–6

This is perhaps not the way that pies are made on the food channels, but if the celebrity chefs were to join you in the bush they would enjoy this meal as much as the food network counterpart.

2 x 400 g rolls frozen puff pastry, defrosted
1 x 50 g sachet tomato paste
$^1/_2$ cup chutney
2 cups cooked curried beef mince
1 onion, peeled, finely chopped and fried in oil
2 cups grated Cheddar cheese
$^1/_4$ cup milk

Spray a hinged braai grid (preferably one with an edge) thoroughly with nonstick cooking spray. Thinly roll out (you can use a rolling pin, a clean bottle or a can from your ammo box) the one packet of pastry, just smaller than the grid and place on the bottom half of the grid. Roll out the remaining pastry a little smaller than the first and set aside. Spread the tomato paste and chutney over the pastry on the grid. Sprinkle the mince, onion and cheese over evenly. Keep the edge of the pastry clear. Place the remaining pastry over the filling. Tightly press the two sheets together, sealing the edges to form a parcel. Close the braai grid and brush the milk over the pastry on both sides. Don't close the grid too tightly, otherwise the pastry and filling will be squeezed out through the gaps in the grid. Place the grid quite high over hot coals so the pastry doesn't burn. Turn it regularly – especially for the first few minutes – so the pastry cooks and doesn't sag through the grid's gaps. Braai for about 30 minutes or until golden brown. Cut it into pieces and tuck into a homemade pie in the middle of nowhere.

Tip: Hurry, hurry is a good name for this pie because if you don't hurry once the pastry is put on the grid, you'll end up with strings of pastry hanging through the grid's gaps!

Ostrich steaks with honey-mustard marinade

Serves 4

This marinade gives a great taste to any steak, whether it's beef or ostrich.

juice of 1 lime or lemon
1 tablespoon honey
1 tablespoon wholegrain mustard
500 g ostrich steaks
olive oil for frying

Mix the lime or lemon juice, honey and mustard together and pour over the steaks. Marinate in the fridge for at least 1 hour. Fry the steaks in the olive oil in a pan or grill over hot coals. Serve with a rice or pasta salad.

Sausage with apple rings

Serves 6

Sausage and apples eaten together? Be adventurous and try this recipe, you won't regret it!

2 tablespoons oil
1 onion, peeled and finely chopped
1 x 250 g packet bacon, diced
2 green apples, peeled, cored and cut into thick slices
6 firm pieces of leftover braai sausage, cut up into small pieces
1 beef stock cube, dissolved in 1 cup boiling water
1 tomato, diced
1 x 420 g can peas (lentils, baked beans or mealies also go well with this recipe)
1 x 100 ml tub plain yoghurt (optional)

Heat the oil and fry the onion and bacon until cooked. Remove the onion and bacon from the pan. Fry the apples on both sides and stir continuously for a few minutes until light brown. Add the onion, bacon, sausage, beef stock, tomato and peas. Cook for a few minutes until the beef stock has reduced and the sauce is nice and thick. Stir in the yoghurt, and tuck in.

Ostrich bobotie
Serves 4

Traditionally, this bobotie recipe is made with beef mince, but try it with ostrich mince instead.

1 thick slice white bread, crusts removed, soaked in 1 cup milk
1 onion, peeled and chopped
1 garlic clove, peeled and crushed
2 tablespoons oil
500 g ostrich mince
1 green apple, grated
1 teaspoon turmeric
1 tablespoon curry powder
1 tablespoon white wine vinegar
1 tablespoon apricot jam
$^1/_4$ cup seedless raisins
1 teaspoon salt
$^1/_2$ teaspoon pepper
1 teaspoon ground coriander
1 teaspoon ground ginger
2 eggs
3 bay leaves

Squeeze the milk out of the bread into a bowl and keep it for later use. Fry the onion and garlic in the oil in a pot until the onion is soft, and then add the mince and stir until it is separated. Now add the apple, turmeric and curry and stir for a few minutes. Add the vinegar, jam, raisins, salt, pepper, coriander, ginger and bread to the mixture, stir through and spoon into a greased fireproof dish. Place a wire rack into a cast-iron pot. Place the bobotie onto the wire rack in the pot and bake for about 20 minutes over moderate coals. In the meantime, beat the milk and eggs together. Remove the lid and slowly pour the milk mixture over the bobotie. Push the bay leaves into the bobotie, put the lid back on and bake for another 20 minutes or until the custard layer has set. Remember to place hot coals on the lid of the pot.

Zorba's moussaka

Serves 6

A good moussaka requires time and effort because you have to prepare quite a few things: first the mince, then the béchamel sauce and you have to fry the potatoes and aubergine. But it's worth it. Use a good red wine for this recipe.

Moussaka
±1 cup olive oil
1 large onion, peeled and chopped
500 g beef mince
4 ripe tomatoes, peeled and chopped
1 x 50 g sachet tomato paste
1 cup red wine
2 teaspoons ground cinnamon
1 teaspoon ground allspice
1 teaspoon dried oregano
   (or 1 tablespoon chopped fresh oregano)
1 teaspoon dried parsley
   (or 1 tablespoon chopped fresh parsley)
1 teaspoon salt
freshly ground black pepper

2 medium aubergines, ends removed
   and sliced lengthways
2 potatoes, peeled and thinly sliced

Béchamel sauce
3 tablespoons butter
4 cups milk
4 tablespoons cake flour
$^1/_2$ teaspoon salt
2 egg yolks
4 tablespoons grated Parmesan
   (or grated Cheddar)
extra grated Parmesan
   (or grated Cheddar) for the topping

To make the mince: Heat 3 tablespoons of oil in a pan and fry the onion until soft. Add the mince, fry until brown and stir continuously to separate the meat. Add the remaining ingredients, up to and including the pepper, to the mince and simmer, covered, over low heat for 1 hour. Stir occasionally to ensure it doesn't dry out or catch. In the meantime, make the vegetables. Fry the aubergines and potatoes in separate batches in the remaining oil until cooked and browned, and spoon onto paper towels to drain.

For the sauce: Melt the butter over low heat, then add the milk, flour and salt. Keep the heat low and whisk continuously to prevent lumps. Simmer for 2–3 minutes and remove from the heat. Stir in the egg yolks and the grated cheese. Place the aubergines in the bottom of a round serving dish, then add a layer of mince, followed by the potatoes and another layer of mince. Pour the sauce on top. Sprinkle extra cheese over. At home, bake for 30 minutes at 180 °C and in the bush you only need to let it stand for 15 minutes.

Sauces

Easy gravy
Serves 4

This gravy goes well with any kind of meat but it is particularly nice with chicken breasts or leg of lamb and rice.

2 tablespoons butter
1 tablespoon cake flour
1 chicken or beef stock cube, dissolved in 1 cup
    boiling water
salt and pepper to taste

Melt the butter in a small saucepan and stir in the flour until it's smooth and starts turning light brown. Slowly add the stock while stirring continuously with a whisk so it doesn't go lumpy. Simmer for a minute or two. Taste whether the gravy is salty enough and season to taste.

Braai sauce
Serves 6–8

We all have our favourite braai sauce to spice up the chops and pap. This tomato-based one is easy, fail-safe and everyone will love it.

2 tablespoons oil
2 onions, peeled and chopped
2 garlic cloves, peeled and chopped
2 tomatoes, peeled and chopped
1 apple, peeled, cored and grated (optional)
1 x 50 g sachet tomato paste
1/2 cup seedless sultanas
1/2 cup dry white wine
1 beef stock cube, dissolved in 1 cup boiling water
1/4 cup chutney
2 tablespoons Worcestershire sauce
2 teaspoons paprika
1 tablespoon apricot jam
salt and pepper to taste

Heat the oil and fry the onions and garlic until golden brown. Add the tomatoes and stir for a minute or two. Add the apple, tomato paste, sultanas, wine, stock, chutney, Worcestershire sauce, paprika and jam and simmer over very low heat for about 30 minutes. Taste whether the stock cube has added sufficient salt before adding seasoning.

Pepper sauce
Serves 4–6

I have yet to encounter someone who doesn't like a thick pepper sauce on a steak. This is an easy, tasty recipe that you can rustle up in no time.

1 x 380 g can Ideal milk
1 tablespoon cornflour, mixed with $1/2$ cup Ideal milk
    taken from the 380 g can Ideal milk listed above
2 tablespoons ground peppercorns
salt to taste

Heat the remaining Ideal milk in a small saucepan. The moment it starts bubbling, add the cornflour mixture and stir with a whisk so it doesn't form lumps. Simmer for 1–2 minutes and then add the peppercorns. If you prefer a thicker sauce, add another tablespoon of cornflour. Remember that the sauce thickens when it cools, so serve it the moment it's ready. Season to taste.

Sweet-and-sour sauce
Serves 6

This sauce is best served with a leg of pork or chicken strips, but you could also serve it with a colourful vegetable stir-fry and basmati rice.

1 tablespoon oil
1 cup finely diced fresh or canned pineapple
1 small red pepper, seeded and cubed
3 tablespoons white wine vinegar
2 teaspoons ground ginger
$1^1/2$ tablespoons brown sugar
$1/2$ tablespoon tomato sauce
2 tablespoons cornflour, mixed with $1/2$ cup cold water
$1^1/2$ teaspoons soy sauce
$1/2$ teaspoon salt
$1^1/2$ cups water
1 tablespoon finely chopped spring onions or
    coriander leaves or parsley (whichever is available,
    or use dried herbs)

Heat the oil. Sauté the pineapple and then stir in the red pepper, vinegar, ginger, brown sugar, tomato sauce, cornflour mixture, soy sauce, salt and water. Simmer over low heat for 5 minutes while stirring continuously. Remove from the heat and sprinkle the spring onions or coriander leaves or parsley over the sauce.

Tip: You can replace the pineapple with 1 cup pineapple juice if you prefer. Taste the sauce when it's done and season to taste. If you prefer it more sour, add vinegar, and if you prefer it sweeter, add more brown sugar.

Easy caramel sauce

Serves 6

You will not find a faster and easier or even tastier recipe than this one. Delicious served with pancakes or any dessert.

1 x 360 g can Nestlé Caramel Treat®
$^1/_4$ cup milk
$^1/_2$ cup nuts (any kind), roughly chopped

Whisk together the Caramel Treat® and milk. When the mixture is smooth, add the nuts and stir through.

Tip: Place some mixed canned fruit on top of a pancake and drizzle this sauce over. It can also be enjoyed with bananas.

Chocolate sauce

Serves 6

Nowadays most people take a freezer along into the bush, so chances are that there'll be ice cream when you pitch camp in the Central Kalahari. Serve this rich chocolate sauce with vanilla ice cream.

1 tablespoon butter
1 cup castor sugar
1 x 250 ml container long-life cream
1 x 100 g slab Lindt chocolate (70% cocoa), roughly broken into blocks

Place a double boiler or any small pot that fits into a bigger one on a hot gas plate. Pour boiling water into the bottom pot and fit the smaller one over it. The water shouldn't touch the base of the top pot. Spoon the butter, sugar and cream into the top saucepan and cover. Leave until the butter and sugar have melted and the mixture is hot. Add the chocolate blocks, but do not stir the sauce. When the chocolate has melted, stir the sauce through once to combine all the ingredients.

Pastas

Colourful pasta salad
Serves 4

This makes a tasty and filling main course for lunch or a side dish for a braai.

¹/₂ x 500 g packet pasta shells
about 20 yellow cherry tomatoes, halved
about 20 red cherry tomatoes, halved
about ¹/₄ English cucumber, diced
1 x 200 g packet pitted black olives, drained
1 garlic clove, peeled and crushed
¹/₂ cup olive oil
4 tablespoons red or white wine vinegar
2 tablespoons chopped spring onions
2 tablespoons dried basil
salt and pepper to taste

Boil the pasta uncovered in salted water in a pot until *al dente* (firm but not hard). Drain as soon as it's cooked and put the pasta in a large serving bowl. Add the tomatoes, cucumber and olives. Mix the garlic, olive oil and vinegar together and stir through the salad. Sprinkle the spring onions and basil over and season to taste.

Tip: If you can't take fresh herbs along to the bush, you can use dried herbs. Just halve the given quantities of the fresh herbs.

Macaroni milk pudding
Serves 6

There's nothing like the smell of cinnamon sugar when you're cold and tired. This recipe is perfect for those chilly and rainy days when your safari people need a pick-me-up.

1 cup macaroni
4 cups milk
¹/₄ cup white sugar
¹/₄ teaspoon salt
2 tablespoons butter
¹/₄ cup custard powder
2 tablespoons cake flour
cinnamon sugar (cinnamon mixed with sugar)

Boil the macaroni in water until *al dente* and drain. Heat 3 cups of milk to boiling point and add the sugar, salt and butter. Don't make the gas plate too hot because the milk mixture catches and burns easily. Mix the custard powder, cake flour and the remaining cup of milk together and stir until smooth. Stir the custard mixture into the boiled milk until the mixture starts thickening. Lower the heat, add the cooked macaroni and let it simmer for 5 minutes. Spoon into bowls, sprinkle generously with cinnamon sugar and eat immediately.

Tip: As a dessert this is enough for six people, but as lunch it will be enough for four hungry stomachs.

Pasta and ragu meat sauce

Serves 6

Don't be intimidated by the name; it's actually just a bolognaise sauce.

2 tablespoons oil
1 onion, peeled and chopped
1 celery stick, chopped
1 carrot, peeled and chopped
500 g mince
$^{1}/_{2}$ cup dry white wine
1 x 400 g can whole Italian tomatoes
1 teaspoon salt
1 teaspoon white pepper
1 x 500 g packet tagliatelle pasta

Heat the oil and fry the onion, celery and carrot until the onion is soft. Add the mince and fry until brown. Add the white wine and stir for 5 minutes. Add the tomatoes and mash them with a wooden spoon while stirring. Cover the saucepan and let the sauce simmer over low heat for 2–3 hours. Ensure the liquid doesn't boil away; should this happen, add a little water. Season to taste after the sauce has finished cooking. In the meantime cook the pasta in salted water until *al dente*. Serve the pasta with the meat sauce.

Tip: As the sauce has to simmer for 2–3 hours, it's better to make it at home beforehand and take it along on safari in your camp freezer. It won't take up much packing space.

Rasta pasta

Serves 6–8

This recipe is named after the red, yellow and green colours of the sweet peppers it contains. If you can't or don't want to take fresh sweet peppers along, a bottle of the preserved or pickled variety works just as well.

1 x 500 g packet three-colour pasta (any type)
3 tablespoons oil
1 onion, peeled and thinly sliced
3 sweet peppers (green, red and yellow), seeded and
    thinly sliced
1 teaspoon chilli flakes
2 cups diced cooked chicken
1 cup long-life cream
125 g Simonzola cheese (or any other blue cheese),
    broken into small pieces

Cook the pasta in plenty of salted water until *al dente*. Meanwhile, heat the oil in a pan and fry the onion until soft. Add the sweet peppers and stir-fry quickly – if you fry them for too long, they will become soggy and look wilted. Add the chilli flakes, chicken, cream and cheese and simmer over low heat for 2–3 minutes until the cheese has melted. Drain the cooked pasta. Mix the pasta and the sauce together.

Pumpkin lasagna

Serves 4

You can also use this filling in cannelloni tubes or pancakes, or simply eat it on its own.
The lemon zest makes it a winner.

White sauce
1 tablespoon butter
1 tablespoon cake flour
1 cup milk
a pinch of salt

Lasagna
2 cups cooked mashed pumpkin or
    butternut

finely grated zest of 1 lemon
1 egg
1 x 214 g tub ricotta cheese (a little more
    or less won't matter)
salt and pepper to taste
9 sheets of lasagna (the number depends
    on the size of bowl you're using; enough
    for about three layers)
dried parsley to garnish

For the white sauce: Melt the butter in a small saucepan. Add the flour and stir. Now add the milk bit by bit. Whisk continuously to stop lumps from forming. Season to taste and leave to simmer over low heat for 2 minutes.

To make the lasagna: Mix the pumpkin, lemon zest, egg, ricotta and salt and pepper together. Boil the lasagna sheets for 10 minutes in a pot with water and a little oil so the sheets don't stick together. Loosen the sheets with two forks as soon as they start sticking. Remove and drain well. Spoon a layer of the pumpkin mixture into a greased dish, place a single layer of lasagna sheets on top and then cover with a thin layer of white sauce. Continue layering until all the ingredients are finished, but end with the white sauce. If you plan on baking the lasagna in an oven, preheat it to 180 °C and bake for 1 hour. Let it stand for another hour so that the lasagna can set. Sprinkle parsley on top for colour. If you plan on baking it on an open fire, use a flat-bottomed cast-iron pot with a wire grid that fits inside. (They're readily available, but you can also use the grids you get with an electric frying pan.) Place the lasagna dish on this grid and cover. Place the pot on moderate coals (so it doesn't burn) and pack a few coals on the lid. Bake as above.

Tip: You can replace the ricotta with crumbled feta if preferred. And for variation you can also spoon a little tomato relish over the lasagna.

Worm sausages

Adapt the number of ingredients according to the number of people who will be enjoying this fun and easy meal. This recipe travelled all over cyberspace a while ago. It works like a charm and the kids (and even the dads) will love it!

red or vienna sausages, quartered
raw spaghetti, broken in half
tomato sauce

Carefully thread six pieces of spaghetti through each sausage quarter. Bring a pot of water to a rapid boil. Place the sausages in the water one by one. This is done so that the water keeps on boiling and doesn't suddenly cool down when you add everything simultaneously. Boil for 15 minutes (if you boil it for a shorter time, the spaghetti inside the sausages won't be properly cooked). Serve with tomato sauce.

Ostrich steak strips on pasta
Serves 4

This pasta is so tasty you can patent the recipe in Rome and make stacks of money.

1 tablespoon butter
2 tablespoons olive oil
1 onion, peeled and chopped
1 garlic clove, peeled and crushed
500 g ostrich steaks, cut into strips
1 carrot, peeled and finely diced
1 x 50 g sachet tomato paste
$1/2$ cup good red wine
1 beef stock cube, dissolved in 1 cup boiling water
freshly ground black pepper

Heat the butter and oil in a large pan. Fry the onion and garlic until soft. Add the meat and stir until it has browned. Stir in the carrot, then the tomato paste, wine and the beef stock. Cover and let the meat simmer over very low heat for 1 hour. Watch the sauce to ensure that it doesn't burn and that it is thick enough when it is cooked. If not, remove the lid and let it boil over high heat until the sauce has thickened. Remove the pot from the heat and taste whether it needs salt (usually the beef stock makes it salty enough). Season with freshly ground black pepper. Serve with spaghetti and grated Parmesan.

Tip: The Italians don't drown their pasta in sauce. If the pasta is too dry to your taste, add a can of chopped tomatoes to make it more saucy.

Vegetarian mains

Stuffed peppers
Serves 4

If you can braai meat, you can braai veggies too. Beware, the meat eaters might just end up eating all your vegetables.

4 tablespoons olive oil
$^1/_2$ cup raw rice
1 garlic clove, peeled and crushed
1 vegetable stock cube, dissolved in 1 cup boiling water
1 punnet chives, ends cut off and finely chopped, or a tablespoon of dried chives
10 cherry tomatoes, halved
12 black olives, pitted
a few fresh basil leaves or basil pesto
4 large red peppers
heavy-duty foil

Heat the oil in a pan and fry the rice for a few minutes while stirring continuously. Add the garlic and stir for another minute or two. Add the prepared stock, cover and turn the gas down low so that the rice can simmer slowly until it's cooked and all the water has boiled off. Add water if the rice boils dry before it's cooked. Add the chives, tomatoes, black olives and basil to the rice. The chicken stock is already salty so you needn't add salt. Cut the stems off the peppers and keep the 'lid' for later. Remove the pips with a sharp knife and spoon – be careful not to break the pepper casing. Spoon the rice filling into the peppers and lightly replace the 'lid'. Depending on the size of the peppers any leftover rice filling can be used in a salad or incorporated into another dish. Cut four large squares of heavy-duty foil and wrap each pepper in it. Braai the foil parcels on a grid over moderate coals for 20 minutes while turning them over at regular intervals. At home you can bake the parcels in the oven at 180 °C. Serve immediately, otherwise the peppers go soft.

Fried haloumi and asparagus

Serves 4

Not all vegetarians eat animal by-products such as cheese and eggs. This is a great starter for meat eaters as well as those vegetarians who eat cheese. The fabulous sauce can be served with any vegetables.

Sauce
zest and juice of 1 lemon
1 tablespoon red wine vinegar
1 small garlic clove, peeled and crushed
1 teaspoon wholegrain mustard
2 tablespoons finely chopped coriander
    leaves (or coriander pesto)
2 tablespoons olive oil
a pinch of salt
a pinch of freshly ground black pepper

Haloumi and asparagus
olive oil for frying
a handful of fresh or canned asparagus
    (more, if you are making this recipe as
    a main course)
1/4 cup cake flour
1/4 teaspoon salt
freshly ground black pepper
400 g haloumi, thickly sliced

For the sauce: Mix all the sauce ingredients together and set aside for later use.

For the haloumi and asparagus: Heat some olive oil in two pans. Cut off the bottom ends of the asparagus and fry in one of the pans. Turn often with braai tongs so that they fry on all sides. The asparagus should be done but still firm. Mix the cake flour, salt and pepper and lightly roll the haloumi in the flour mixture. Fry each slice in the second pan until golden brown. Keep the heat moderate so it doesn't burn. It only takes a minute or two to brown. Remove from the pan and place on paper towels to drain. Place the asparagus on plates, arrange the haloumi slices on top and drizzle the sauce over. Serve immediately with a French loaf and a glass of chilled wine.

Chickpea burgers

Serves 6

Chickpeas are an important part of vegetarian meals. Not only are they tasty but also filling and extremely versatile.

1 x 400 g can chickpeas, drained and rinsed
3 medium carrots, peeled and finely grated
1 small onion, peeled and finely grated
1 x 120 g tub hummus or tahini (chickpea or sesame spread)
1 egg
2 slices whole-wheat bread, crumbed
1 teaspoon ground cumin
1 teaspoon salt
1/2 teaspoon white pepper
3 tablespoons olive oil
1/2 cup unflavoured soy yoghurt or plain yoghurt
zest of 1 lemon and 1 teaspoon lemon juice
6 hamburger rolls
1 avocado, mashed with a pinch of salt

Mash the chickpeas as finely as you can with a potato masher. Add the carrots, onion, 2 tablespoons of hummus, the egg, breadcrumbs, cumin, salt and pepper. Mix well and divide into six equal portions. Shape each portion into a burger patty, cover and refrigerate for 1 hour. Fry the patties in olive oil until they're golden brown. Mix the yoghurt with the remaining hummus (or tahini), the lemon zest and lemon juice. Spread the yoghurt mixture on the bread rolls. Divide the mashed avocado among the rolls and place a burger on each roll. You can also add lettuce, tomato, spring onion or any other salad ingredient.

Chickpea stew

Serves 4–6

Recently a global request was made for at least one meat-free day during the week. Once you have tasted this mouthwatering stew it will be easier to have your own meat-free day every week.

3 tablespoons oil
2 onions, peeled and chopped
2 garlic cloves, peeled and chopped
1/2 teaspoon ground cumin
1/2 teaspoon turmeric
1/2 teaspoon ground cinnamon
1/2 teaspoon ground ginger
1/2 teaspoon ground coriander
1/2 teaspoon curry powder
1/2 teaspoon dried parsley
1/2 teaspoon sugar
1 cup sliced mixed vegetables
2 x 400 g cans chickpeas, drained and rinsed
1 x 400 g can tomato-and-onion mix
1 vegetable stock cube, dissolved in 1 cup boiling water
salt and pepper to taste

Heat the oil and fry the onions and garlic until golden brown. Add the rest of the ingredients. Simmer slowly for 30 minutes, checking every now and then to ensure there's enough liquid in the pot. If it is too watery for your taste, remove the lid and let it boil rapidly until the liquid has reduced. Serve with rice.

Curried eggs

Serves 4

If you want to make a quick meal then this is the recipe for you! This forgotten golden oldie will have everyone thinking that you created a divine new recipe!

4 tablespoons olive oil
1 large onion, peeled and chopped
1 green apple, peeled, cored and diced
2 tablespoons cake flour
1 tablespoon curry powder
1 tablespoon ground cumin
1 tablespoon smooth apricot jam
2 tablespoons chutney
1 cup chicken stock
6 hard-boiled eggs, shells removed and halved

Heat the olive oil in a pan and fry the onion until soft. Add the apple and fry for another 2–3 minutes. Stir in the flour, curry powder, cumin, apricot jam and chutney. Gradually add the chicken stock while stirring continuously until the sauce is thick. Place the egg halves in a bowl and pour the sauce over. Traditionally, curry eggs are served with rice and a salad, but in the bundu, pot bread will also work well.

Variation: Replace the apple with 3–4 small bananas, sliced lengthways.

Vegetarian curry

Serves 4

Of course you needn't be a vegetarian to try this recipe – you might like it so much that you decide not to have meat at least once a week.

1 large onion, peeled and chopped
2 tablespoons oil
1 tablespoon ground ginger
1 tablespoon ground cumin
1 tablespoon ground coriander
1 tablespoon curry powder, or less if you prefer
  it milder
1 x 400 g can lentils, drained and rinsed
1 x 400 g can chickpeas, drained and rinsed
1 x 400 g can chopped tomatoes
1 x 400 g can coconut milk
salt and pepper to taste

Fry the onion in oil until soft. Add the spices and curry powder and stir for a minute or two. Add the rest of the ingredients and simmer gently for 10 minutes.

Tip: You can steam two handfuls of spinach in a separate pot, drain it and add it to the curry.

Vegetables

Potatoes with pesto
Serves 4

An easy recipe that can be served hot or cold.

20 baby potatoes or 5 standard potatoes, quartered
10 cherry tomatoes, halved or 2 large tomatoes, diced
$^1/_2$ cup basil pesto
$^1/_2$ cup buttermilk (you can use milk if you can't get
   buttermilk)
salt to taste
freshly ground black pepper

Boil the potatoes in a pot of salted water until soft. Drain and set aside to cool a little. Peel and halve the potatoes, then place them in a bowl together with the tomatoes. Mix the pesto, buttermilk or milk and salt together and pour this mixture over the potatoes. Sprinkle black pepper over and serve.

Potatoes with lemon zest
Serves 8

Try these oil-fried potatoes – they taste just like baked potatoes, and the lemon zest gives this side dish a special tang.

8–10 potatoes, peeled and quartered
oil for deep-frying
salt to taste
finely grated zest of 1 lemon – ensure you only grate
   the yellow and not the bitter white part of the peel

Dry the potatoes with a paper towel or a clean dishcloth. Heat the oil in a deep pot until hot — when you add the potatoes, the oil should start bubbling immediately otherwise it is not hot enough. Fry four potato quarters at a time until golden brown outside and cooked inside. (If you cook too many potatoes simultaneously they won't crisp.) Do not let the oil get too hot during the cooking process. Keep the cooked potatoes warm in a dish placed over a saucepan of boiling water. As soon as all the potatoes have been fried, sprinkle some salt and the lemon zest over. The potatoes are esspecially tasty with the Greek leg of lamb (see page 56).

Tip: You can boil the potatoes in salted water until only just soft, before frying them in the oil. This will ensure the potatoes are soft inside and crispy outside.

Sweet potato-and-spinach filling

Serves 4–6

This fragrant filling tastes as if it was specially made for pancakes but can be enjoyed on its own as well.

4 tablespoons oil
1 onion, peeled and finely chopped
2 garlic cloves, peeled and crushed
1 teaspoon curry powder
2 cups peeled and cubed sweet potatoes
1 x 50 g sachet tomato paste
2 cups vegetable stock
$^1/_2$ teaspoon chilli flakes
1 teaspoon ground ginger
1 tablespoon brown sugar
4 large handfuls young spinach leaves, washed
1–2 tablespoons smooth peanut butter
1 tablespoon ground coriander
salt and pepper to taste

Heat the oil in a pot and fry the onion and garlic until soft. Stir in the curry powder and fry for 1 minute. Add the sweet potatoes, stirring for about 3 minutes to ensure that they are coated in the mixture. Add the tomato paste, vegetable stock, chilli flakes, ginger and brown sugar. Simmer over low heat until the sweet potatoes are cooked. Add the spinach leaves, stir and simmer for 1 minute. Finally, add the peanut butter and then the coriander and salt and pepper to taste (be mindful of adding salt because usually the stock is salty enough).

Mealie fritters

Serves 6

Mealie fritters are one of those side dishes that complements almost any main meal. They can also be served for breakfast, especially if combined with crispy bacon and honey.

2 eggs, separated
1 x 415 g can creamed sweet corn
$^3/_4$ cup cake flour
$^1/_2$ teaspoon baking powder
$^1/_4$ teaspoon salt
oil for deep-frying

Beat the egg whites until stiff peaks form. Mix the rest of the ingredients, except the oil, together in another bowl and fold in the egg whites. Heat the oil in a pan and, when hot, drop tablespoonsful of the mixture into the oil. Fry the fritters until brown on both sides, then drain on paper towels to soak up the oil. Serve hot. The great thing about this meal is that these fritters can also be served cold as *padkos*.

Mealies on the coals

Serves 6

Fresh mealies (corn on the cob) are synonymous with summer. This recipe will become a firm fixture on your calendar.

6 mealies (corn on the cob), stripped and broken
   into smaller pieces or kept whole
$1/2$ teaspoon salt (plus $1/2$ teaspoon salt for the sauce)
$1/2$ cup olive oil
juice of $1/2$ lemon
1 garlic clove, peeled and finely chopped (optional)
$1/2$ teaspoon prepared mustard

Boil the mealies in salted water until cooked, drain and set aside to cool. (You can also cook them the previous night so they're ready to chuck onto the coals.) Arrange the mealies on a large piece of heavy-duty foil, shiny side facing inwards, and turn the edges upward. Mix the remaining ingredients together and pour the sauce over the mealies. Close the foil carefully and place the mealie parcels in a folding braai grid. Thirty minutes over mild coals should do the trick. Turn the grid occasionally to distribute the heat evenly.

Pumpkin fritters

Serves 6–8

The pecan nuts and feta cheese make these pumpkin fritters really special.

2 cups cooked mashed pumpkin or butternut
1 cup cake flour
1 teaspoon baking powder
2 eggs, beaten
$1/2$ cup pecan nuts, chopped
oil for frying
1 round of feta cheese, crumbled
2 teaspoons ground cinnamon
$1/2$ cup honey

Mix the pumpkin, flour, baking powder, eggs and pecan nuts together. Heat a little oil in a pan and drop dollops of batter into it. Fry on both sides until golden brown and cooked. Drain the fritters on paper towels and keep warm. Layer the pumpkin fritters on a platter and sprinkle feta cheese and cinnamon over each layer. Drizzle honey over and serve warm.

Tip: You can serve the fritters on a platter or as individual servings, both work well.

Green pumpkin peel

Serves 4

Have you ever eaten a pumpkin peel that tastes just like green beans, only better? If you are lucky enough to find a fresh Hubbard squash you should try this delicious recipe! The pumpkin must be young and fresh though!

3 cups finely sliced fresh Hubbard squash peels
1 large potato, peeled and cubed
1 onion, peeled and chopped
1 teaspoon salt

Cook all the ingredients together in water over medium heat until the potato is soft. Mash all the ingredients together to combine, and serve.

Sweet potatoes with cream cheese

Serves 4

Sweet potatoes are a real stalwart on any safari because they stay fresh for a long time and you can make lots of tasty meals with them.

foil (enough for 4 parcels)
4 large sweet potatoes, washed and dried
oil
salt to taste
1 x 230 g tub low-fat cream cheese (Sweet Thai Chilli flavour works well)
a few caper berries (see tip)

Cover each sweet potato and the inner layer of foil lightly with oil. Sprinkle salt over the sweet potatoes and fold the foil to seal the parcel. Bake for 30 minutes on the grid over low to medium-hot coals or until the sweet potato is soft (first test one sweet potato by inserting a sharp knife — if the knife cuts through easily the sweet potatoes are ready). Remove the sweet potatoes from the foil. Being careful not to cut right through, slice slits into each sweet potato. (You can also cut the sweet potatoes before wrapping them up in the foil.) Insert cream cheese into every slit and place a few caper berries on top.

Tip: Caper berries are not nasturtium seeds. They are the half-ripe fruit of the caper bush that have been soaked in vinegar. If you can't find them, you can use olives, sun-dried tomatoes, Peppadews® or pieces of pineapple.

Tomato pumpkin

Serves 6

You won't believe how tasty this dish is, especially when served with a juicy steak done over the coals.

1 x 500 g packet peeled pumpkin cubes
$^1/_2$ cup sugar
$^1/_2$ cup water
2 tablespoons butter
1 large onion, peeled and chopped
1 x 400 g can chopped Italian tomatoes
3 slices white bread, crumbed
$^1/_2$ cup milk
1 egg
1 teaspoon salt
$^1/_2$ teaspoon ground black pepper
1 cup grated Cheddar cheese

Place the pumpkin, sugar, water and half the butter in a pot and simmer over low heat until all the liquid has cooked away and the pumpkin is dry and soft. At the end of the cooking process the pumpkin will fry a little in the butter and sugar – stir to stop it from catching, but don't mash the pumpkin cubes. Fry the onion in a separate pot in the remaining butter and then add the tomatoes. Simmer for a few minutes until thick and not watery. Grease a shallow ovenproof dish with butter and sprinkle half of the bread-crumbs over the bottom of the dish. Spoon in the pumpkin and then add the tomatoes. Beat the milk, egg, salt and pepper together and pour it over the tomatoes. Draw a knife along the sides and through the middle of the dish so that the milk mixture can seep through. Mix the rest of the breadcrumbs with the cheese and sprinkle it on top. Bake for 45 minutes, or until it has set. You can either bake it in an oven preheated to 180 °C, or over an open fire – then follow the method used for the pumpkin lasagna (see page 99).

Onion rings

Serves 4

If you're craving steakhouse fare after many days in the bush, make these crispy onion rings.

Batter
1¼ cups self-raising flour
½ teaspoon salt
1 teaspoon paprika
1 cup water

Onions
oil for deep-frying
2 large onions, peeled and cut into rings
½ cup self-raising flour

To make the batter: Mix all the batter ingredients together in a bowl and refrigerate for about 30 minutes.

To make the onion rings: Heat the oil until hot, drop a bit of batter in the oil, if it starts bubbling immediately, the oil is hot enough. Dip the onion rings in the flour and then in the batter. Deep-fry them in small batches until golden brown. Serve immediately.

Volcano potatoes

Serves 4

These potatoes are a real treat and are particularly tasty served with juicy boerewors.

4 large potatoes
½ cup buttermilk (or more if the potatoes aren't creamy enough)
1 teaspoon chopped chives or spring onion (or dried chives)
½ teaspoon mustard powder
2 teaspoons sugar
1 teaspoon salt
freshly ground black pepper
1 teaspoon cayenne pepper or paprika for garnishing

Wash the potatoes, but don't peel them. Boil the potatoes whole until soft. Drain the water and leave the potatoes in the pot until they have cooled sufficiently for you to be able to work with them. (You can also bake the potatoes in foil on the coals.) Cut the potatoes in half lengthways. Spoon out most of the insides, but guard against removing too much of the soft potato; the spuds must still keep their shape. Mix the potato you have removed with the rest of the ingredients and mash everything with a potato masher or fork. Spoon the mixture back into the potato peels and garnish with cayenne pepper or paprika. Serve immediately.

Tip: If you don't have buttermilk use long-life milk.

Salads

Avocado ritz

Serves 4

This starter has been with us for as long as garlic snails and candyfloss. You could replace the shrimps with a can of crab meat or, if you're camping on the Mozambican coast, use fresh crayfish or prawns.

2 ripe, large avocados
chopped lettuce
salt
juice of $1/2$ lemon
1 x 200 g can shrimps
Ina Paarman's Thousand Island salad dressing
freshly ground black pepper
a few pomegranate pips (optional)

Halve the avocados and remove the pips. Peel carefully without breaking. Arrange the lettuce in individual bowls, or on a single plate, place the avocado halves on top and sprinkle a little salt and lemon juice over them. Drain the shrimps well and divide among the four avocado halves. Drizzle over as much salad dressing as you like and sprinkle with a little more salt and pepper. Garnish with the pomegranate pips. Serve immediately, otherwise the lettuce will wilt and the avocados will discolour.

Biltong-and-pasta salad

Serves 6–8

A refreshing cold salad that can be served for lunch.

Salad
1 cup thinly sliced moist biltong
10 Peppadews®, sliced
$1/2$ cup chopped red onion
1 cup diced cucumber
1 cup feta cheese, cubed
1 x 500 g packet pasta shells, cooked and cooled (see tip)

Salad dressing
3 tablespoons wholegrain mustard
1 tablespoon white wine vinegar or lemon juice
$1/2$ teaspoon sugar
$1/4$ teaspoon salt
$1/2$ cup olive oil
1 teaspoon dried parsley

For the salad: Mix all the salad ingredients together in a large bowl.

For the salad dressing: Mix all the salad dressing ingredients together in another bowl. Pour the salad dressing over the salad, toss and serve.

Tip: Stir a little olive oil through the cooked pasta to stop the pasta shells from sticking to each other.

Blue cheese salad

Serves 6

Blue cheese often gets a bad rap as 'smelly cheese', but once you've tasted this salad with blue cheese salad dressing you'll be singing a different tune.

1 cup soft dried pears, chopped
2 cups cooked, chopped beetroot, or 1 x 405 g box Werda chopped, sliced or grated sweet-and-sour beetroot
$^1/_2$ cup blue cheese salad dressing

No salad could be simpler. Just mix all the ingredients together, serve, and graciously accept the compliments.

Variation: Lightly fry the pears in butter before mixing them with the beetroot.

Bread-and-tomato salad

Serves 4–6

If you regard a salad as little more than a side dish, think again. This tomato salad is more than just a salad; it's a meal on its own. And it's remarkably fragrant for something that is this healthy.

3 ciabatta rolls
30 cherry tomatoes at room temperature, halved
2 tablespoons capers
1 red onion, peeled and sliced
1 x 280 g jar roast peppers in olive oil, drained
1 tablespoon red wine vinegar
olive oil to taste
a few fresh basil leaves, torn or basil pesto (see tip)
salt and pepper to taste

If you like buying semi-baked ciabattas, don't bake them some more, rather use them as is. It's best if the bread has that slightly sticky texture. Cut or tear the bread into bite-sized cubes and place in a large salad bowl. Mix the rest of the ingredients together and add them to the bread. Use your hands to mix the salad properly and ensure that the bread is covered with the olive oil sauce. Serve immediately.

Tip: Fresh basil brightens any meal but if you cannot take fresh basil on your trip then basil pesto is an acceptable second choice.

Salad of roast figs and biltong

Serves 4

Traditionally figs are served with ham, but in the bush biltong is your best option.

Salad dressing
2 tablespoons fresh orange juice
3 tablespoons honey
$^1/_4$ cup olive oil
grated zest of $^1/_2$ orange
salt and pepper to taste

Salad
12 soft, dried figs, halved (you can also use fresh figs)
2 tablespoons olive oil
$^1/_2$ head lettuce, washed and dried
1 orange, peeled, segmented and all the pith removed
$1^1/_2$ cups moist, sliced biltong
water biscuits to serve

For the salad dressing: Whisk all the ingredients together and refrigerate.

For the salad: Place the fig halves on the grid over a medium-hot fire and baste with olive oil. Roast for a few minutes until the figs just start to soften. Arrange the lettuce, orange segments and biltong on four plates and place the lukewarm figs on top. Drizzle the dressing over the salad and serve immediately with the water biscuits.

Cold chicken salad

Serves 4

Use last night's cooked chicken leftovers to create this delicious and beautifully presented salad.

3 cups cubed, cooked chicken
1 cup dried cranberries
$^1/_4$ cup finely chopped red onion
1 apple (any kind), peeled, cored and diced
$^1/_2$ cup chopped pecan nuts
1 cup mayonnaise
1 teaspoon lemon juice
$^1/_2$ teaspoon curry powder
$^1/_4$ teaspoon salt
freshly ground black pepper
$^1/_2$ head lettuce, washed and dried

Mix the chicken, cranberries, onion, apple and nuts in a bowl. Mix the mayonnaise, lemon juice, curry powder, salt and pepper in a separate bowl. Mix the sauce and chicken mixture together and arrange on top of the lettuce on a plate.

Variation: Replace the dried cranberries with cubes of pineapple, soft dried apricots or any other fruit of your choice.

Orange-and-chicken potato salad

Serves 4

Oranges are great on safari as they look pretty and taste great in a salad.

$^1/_2$ head lettuce or baby spinach leaves, washed
   and dried
5 large potatoes, boiled in salt water, peeled
   and quartered
2 oranges, peeled, segmented and pith removed
2 roasted chicken breasts, cubed
$^1/_2$ red onion, peeled and thinly sliced
$^1/_2$ cup honey-and-mustard salad dressing
$^1/_4$ cup finely chopped pecan nuts
thin strips lemon rind for decoration (optional)
freshly ground black pepper

Place the lettuce on a flat serving plate and arrange the potatoes, oranges, chicken and onion on top. Drizzle the salad dressing over, then scatter over the pecan nuts and lemon rind. To finish, grind some black pepper over the salad.

Variation: If you have some fresh mint leaves at hand, cut up a few and sprinkle over the salad.

Couscous salad

Serves 6

A braai with only meat and salad is not a proper braai – you'll need some starch to come to the rescue. This recipe takes no more than a few minutes and you'll shed nary a drop of sweat in preparing it.

3 cups raw couscous
$^1/_2$ teaspoon salt
3 cups boiling water
$^1/_2$ cup canned or frozen green peas
$^1/_2$ cup quartered cherry tomatoes or chopped
   sun-dried tomatoes
3 tablespoons balsamic vinegar
2 tablespoons olive oil
black pepper to taste

Place the couscous in a pot and add the salt and boiling water. Leave to stand, covered, for 10 minutes to absorb all the water. Gently loosen the couscous with a fork and set aside to cool. Add the remaining ingredients and serve.

Variation: If you really want to be snazzy, make an individual salad for each diner, as follows: Lightly coat the insides of six small round plastic tubs with oil. Spoon the couscous into the tubs and press down tightly. Turn the tubs over onto plates and arrange the rest of the food around them. These containers are small and take up very little space, so you needn't leave the jack at home.

Easy bacon-and-egg salad

Serves 6

When you grow tired of the hustle and bustle of the city make this egg salad, pack it into your cooler bag and have a picnic next to a river.

Salad
2 handfuls fresh lettuce, washed, dried and broken into bite-sized chunks
6 hard-boiled eggs, shells removed and sliced into rounds
1 x 250 g packet bacon, fried and cut into smaller pieces
1 red onion, peeled and thinly sliced

Salad dressing
$1/4$ cup chicken stock
1 teaspoon curry powder
2 tablespoons smooth apricot jam
$1/2$ cup mayonnaise
$1/2$ cup plain yoghurt
2 teaspoons dried parsley (or fresh parsley) to ganish

For the salad: Mix all the ingredients together in a bowl.

For the salad dressing: Whisk all the ingredients together, except the parsley. Pour the dressing over the salad, garnish with parsley and serve.

Tip: If you're having the egg salad later, pack the dressing separately from the salad ingredients and only pour over just before serving, otherwise the lettuce will become soggy.

Watermelon kebabs

Serves 6

The fragrant smell of watermelon takes you back to childhood holidays and riverside picnics in the shade of willow trees. You can also use this salad as a starter by using toothpicks instead of kebab skewers with a piece of watermelon, cheese and an olive per skewer.

$1/2$ small watermelon, peeled and cubed
a hefty block of mozzarella cheese, diced
pitted black olives
kebab skewers

Thread the watermelon, cheese and olives onto the kebab skewers, alternating the ingredients. Use one of the hollowed-out halves of the watermelon as a serving dish for the kebabs.

Variation: Instead of threading the ingredients onto skewers, serve them in a salad bowl. You can also replace the mozzarella with feta as feta would crumble if placed on a skewer.

Rice salad with fruit

Serves 6

This scrumptious rice salad is ideal for a special meal on a hot summer's day. It must be eaten on the same day as it is prepared or the pineapple will become soggy.

Rice
2 tablespoons butter
2 teaspoons curry powder
1 cup raw rice
1 teaspoon salt
2 bananas, peeled and sliced
1 pineapple, peeled and grated
$^1/_2$ cup chopped pecan nuts,
   to garnish

Condensed milk sauce
1 teaspoon mustard powder
$^1/_4$ teaspoon salt
$^1/_4$ teaspoon white pepper
1 x 385 g can condensed milk
1 egg yolk
$^1/_4$ cup sunflower oil
$^1/_4$ cup white wine vinegar

For the rice: Melt the butter and stir in the curry powder. Add the rice and fry for a minute or two. Add enough boiling water to cover the rice, add the salt and boil the rice until soft and cooked. Remove from heat and wait until the rice has cooled.

For the sauce: Mix the mustard powder, salt and white pepper together. Stir the mustard powder mixture into the condensed milk. Beat the egg yolk and add it to the condensed milk, followed by the oil and the vinegar. Stir thoroughly before adding each ingredient.

For the salad: Layer the rice, bananas, pineapple and the salad dressing in a bowl (this salad looks good in a glass bowl). End with the salad dressing as the top layer and garnish with pecan nuts.

Sides

Egg snacks
Makes 12 egg snacks

These snacks don't have to be baked or fried and are ideal for enjoying at sunset next to the waterhole.

6 hard-boiled eggs, shells removed
1 cup grated Cheddar cheese
1 x 200 g box Salticrax® biscuits, crushed into
   fine crumbs
mayonnaise, enough to dampen the egg mixture so that
   you can roll it into small balls
1 x 125 g packet potato chips (any flavour), crushed
   into fine crumbs

Wait until the eggs have completely cooled down and then grate them. Add the cheese, Salticrax® crumbs and mayonnaise and mix well. Don't use too much mayonnaise, otherwise the mixture will be too soft. Depending on the type of mayonnaise you use, you should use between $1/4$ and $1/2$ cup. Roll the egg mixture between the palms of your hands into balls, then in the potato chip crumbs. Store them in a flat container in your camp fridge or cool box for 1–2 hours before you plan to eat them. This will ensure that the egg balls are cool and firm. Serve with sweet chilli sauce.

Coconut rice
Serves 4–6

Adding coconut cream to the ingredients is one of the easiest ways to make any meal tasty and exotic. This coconut rice is divine with just about everything, but it goes especially well with prawns, fish and curries.

1 cup raw basmati rice
2 cups boiling water
1 teaspoon salt
1 x 400 g can coconut cream or milk

Add the rice, boiling water and salt to a pot and bring to the boil. Cover and let it simmer for 1 hour over very low heat (it must steam, not boil). Stir in the coconut cream or milk and leave it on the stove or over the coals until it's warmed through and all the liquid has been absorbed.

Tip: Coconut cream is more concentrated than coconut milk, but you can use either one for this recipe.

Couscous

Serves 4

No side dish is as easy, quick and versatile as couscous – so put it at the top of your packing list.

2 cups raw couscous
1 teaspoon salt
2 cups boiling water

Place the couscous and salt in a saucepan and add the boiling water (do not stir). Cover with a lid and let it stand for 10 minutes. Then stir with a fork to separate the grains.

You can serve couscous hot with a stew (instead of rice), or mix it with hot veggies such as cooked cubes of butternut. Or serve it cold with all sorts of salad ingredients. And how about dates and nuts with cream for an exotic dessert?

Traditional yellow rice

Serves 4

Yellow rice isn't something that you eat every day but you will find yourself asking why not, when you taste this mouthwatering side dish. It is traditionally served with bobotie or leg of lamb.

1 cup raw rice
3 cups boiling water
1 teaspoon salt
1 tablespoon sugar
1 teaspoon turmeric
1 cinnamon stick
1 tablespoon butter
1/2 cup seedless raisins

Place all the ingredients in a pot and simmer until the rice is soft and cooked. Remove the cinnamon stick before serving.

Wild banana chips

Serves 4

You can take the kids out of the city, but it's not always possible to take the city out of the kids. If they start talking about their favourite takeaway shop in their sleep, you can dish up this alternative in no time at all. Green wild bananas (plantains) are not bananas that aren't ripe yet, they are more starchy and similar to potatoes or sweet potatoes. You can find them in most African countries and sometimes, if you are lucky, you will spot some in a local supermarket too.

5 small, green wild bananas, peeled (use a sharp knife)
oil for deep-frying
salt to taste

Cut the bananas into long potato-chip-like or round slices. Heat the oil and fry the bananas until golden brown. They soften quickly and burn easily, so watch them. Drain the chips on paper towels, sprinkle with salt, and serve.

Tip: If you can't get hold of green wild bananas, use potatoes or sweet potatoes.

Tomato rice from West Africa

Serves 6

The West Africans love this fragrant rice dish. It is best served with fish, chicken or stuffed aubergine and large brown mushrooms. If children are joining in the meal, you can leave out the chillies, but otherwise … bring it on.

1 x 50 g can anchovies (or use a bit of oil if you
    dislike anchovies)
1 onion, peeled and finely chopped
1 small garlic clove, peeled and chopped
1 teaspoon chilli flakes
1 red pepper, seeded and finely chopped
2 teaspoons curry powder
1 x 690 g bottle Italian tomato purée
1 chicken stock cube, dissolved in 1 cup boiling water
juice of $\frac{1}{2}$ lemon
1 cup raw rice

Pour the anchovies, oil and all, into a saucepan and heat. Stir until the anchovies have disintegrated and then add the onion and garlic. Fry for a few minutes until the onion is soft, and then add the chilli flakes, red pepper and curry powder. Fry for another minute or two. Add the tomato purée, chicken stock, lemon juice and rice. Simmer over low heat until the rice is cooked and most of the liquid has been absorbed. Stir often as it tends to catch. Remove the saucepan from the heat and set aside for 30 minutes to 1 hour, until all the liquid has been absorbed.

Breads and bakes

Basic bread recipe
Makes 1 big pot bread

7 cups white bread flour
2 x 10 g sachets instant yeast
2¹/₂ cups lukewarm water
2 tablespoons sugar
1 tablespoon fine salt

Put the flour in a deep mixing bowl. Mix the yeast, water and sugar in a separate bowl, and set aside for 10 minutes until it starts foaming. Add the yeast mixture to the flour and then add the salt. Blend well. Knead the dough on a lightly floured surface for about 10 minutes or until it is soft and elastic. Place the dough in a bowl. Cover the bowl with cling wrap and a damp kitchen cloth and leave it in a warm place to rise to double its original size. Knead the bread down again for a few seconds and place it in a greased flat-bottomed cast-iron pot (or two bread pans) so it can rise a second time to double its original size. Place the pot onto moderately hot coals and stack hot coals on the lid. After 30 minutes, check that the bread is starting to turn brown, and replace the lid, with new coals on top. The bread should be done after 1 hour. To test if the bread is done, turn it out of the pot and lightly knock on the bottom with your knuckles. The bread should sound hollow and the bottom and sides should be golden brown when it is done. For two pot breads, one with a sweet and the other with a savoury filling, divide the dough into two once you have finished kneading it. Roll into two 2 cm-thick rectangles and place the following fillings on top:

Sweet filling
1 x 200 g jar Nutella® chocolate spread
2 cups hazelnuts or walnuts, whole or chopped
2 bananas, peeled and cut into rounds

Spread the Nutella over the dough and sprinkle the nuts and banana over evenly. Fold the dough lengthways over the filling. Press together the ends of the dough and roll up from a short end to resemble a swiss roll. Grease a flat-bottomed cast-iron pot well and place the dough, open side down into the pot. Place the pot onto lukewarm coals, place a few hot coals onto the lid and bake for 1 hour or until baked through.

Savoury filling
10 slices ham, cubed
2 cups grated Cheddar cheese
2 handfuls basil leaves or 2 teaspoons dried basil
2 cups sliced sun-dried tomatoes (drain if kept in oil)
1 teaspoon salt, plus a little extra
freshly ground black pepper to taste
2 tablespoons olive oil, plus extra to brush over bread
1 teaspoon dried or fresh rosemary

Place the ingredients up to and including the tomatoes on top of the dough. Sprinkle with salt, black pepper and olive oil. Fold the dough lengthways over the filling, press the ends of the dough together and roll up from a short end to resemble a swiss roll. Turn it onto one of the ends. Brush some olive oil and sprinkle salt and rosemary over the top of the bread. Proceed as above.

Cheese scones in a jaffle pan

Makes 6 scones

You can serve these as is, or cut in half with butter and a filling such as grated cheese, jam or anything else you feel like. Crispy bacon works really well. A cup of hot sweet tea goes down well with these scones.

5 tablespoons oil
2 eggs
1¹/₂ cups milk
2 cups cake flour
1 tablespoon baking powder
2 cups finely grated Cheddar cheese
a pinch of salt

Spray the jaffle pan with a little nonstick cooking spray. Mix all the ingredients together lightly. Divide the dough into six equal pieces. Bake the scones one by one over a gas flame until done, turning the jaffle pan regularly. Don't make the gas plate too hot otherwise the scones will burn on the outside and still be raw inside. It takes about 10 minutes per scone to cook.

Basic pancake batter

Makes about 30 pancakes

4 eggs
5 cups water
1 cup sunflower oil (plus extra for frying)
¹/₄ cup white vinegar
1 teaspoon bicarbonate of soda
1 teaspoon salt
4 cups cake flour
4 teaspoons baking powder

Beat the eggs well. Add 1 cup of water and then the oil and vinegar. Mix the bicarbonate of soda, salt and flour with the remaining water and slowly beat this mixture into the vinegar mixture. Stir in the baking powder. Leave the batter in your camp fridge for at least 1 hour before making the pancakes. Heat a little oil in a pan over moderate coals (or on a gas stove) and pour a thin layer of the pancake batter into the pan. Fry each pancake for 15–20 seconds a side. Keep the cooked pancakes warm by placing them on a plate over a pot filled with hot water. When cooked through, the pancakes won't stick to one another, but it also helps if you first sprinkle sugar on the pancakes when stacking them up (that is, if you're making sweet pancakes).

A few ideas for pancake fillings:

Biltong and grated cheese
Chicken livers in a peri-peri sauce
Leftover bobotie and chutney
Ham and Gruyère cheese
Crispy bacon with maple syrup (you can mix the bacon into the dough or you can use it as a filling)
Boerewors (sausage) or frankfurters with mustard
Salmon and crème fraîche or cottage cheese

Raisin bread

Makes 1 pot bread or 1 large or 2 small loaves

You can stuff your face with this bread when it's freshly baked, and the next day you can use the leftovers for French toast or bread pudding. Raisin bread is the perfect Easter holiday companion.

3/4 cup lukewarm water
1 x 10 g sachet instant yeast
1/4 cup white sugar (plus another 1/2 cup for the filling)
2 eggs, beaten
2 teaspoons salt
1/4 cup soft butter (plus another tablespoon melted butter to spread on the bread)
1 cup seedless raisins
1 cup lukewarm milk (plus 2 tablespoons extra to brush over the dough)
6 cups cake flour
1 tablespoon ground cinnamon

Put the water, yeast and 1 tablespoon sugar in a small bowl and set aside for 10 minutes until it starts foaming. In the meantime, mix together the eggs, 3 tablespoons sugar, salt, butter, raisins and milk. Add the yeast mixture as soon as it starts to foam. Place the flour in a big mixing bowl and add the liquid mixture. Stir through thoroughly, then remove the ball of dough. Sprinkle some flour on a flat surface and place the dough on top. Knead it for about 10 minutes by rolling, pinching, pressing and folding until it's soft and easy to handle. Place the dough in a big greased bowl and cover with cling wrap and a damp kitchen towel. Leave it in a warm place for about 1 hour until the dough has doubled in size. Remove the dough from the bowl and roll it out until it's about 1 cm thick. Mix the 1/2 cup sugar and cinnamon together. Brush the 2 tablespoons milk over the dough and sprinkle with the sugar-and-cinnamon mixture. Grease a flat-bottomed cast-iron pot with butter and roll the dough up tightly from the short side to resemble a swiss roll. Place the dough in the pot. If you want to make two long loaves of bread, cut the dough in half. Spread the extra melted butter over the dough and let it stand in a warm place for about 1 hour or until it has doubled in size again. Bake in the pot for 1 hour, or until done, over moderate coals.

Health loaf

Makes 1 pot bread or 2 loaves

This wholesome bread is quick and easy to prepare.

2 heaped teaspoons bicarbonate of soda
1 cup brown sugar or honey
3 x 500 ml tubs plain yoghurt
6 cups Nutty Wheat® flour
4 cups brown bread flour
1 1/2 cups bran
2 teaspoons salt

Mix the bicarbonate of soda and brown sugar or honey with the yoghurt and stir until it has dissolved. Blend all the dry ingredients together. Add the yoghurt mixture and mix well. Bake for 1 1/2 hours over moderate coals in a black cast-iron pot or two greased bread pans.

Pumpkin *vetkoek*

Makes 10–15 *vetkoek*

Are these vetkoek with pumpkin or pumpkin fritters that contain too much flour? Decide for yourself ...

2 cups cake flour
2 teaspoons baking powder
1 tablespoon sugar
2 eggs, beaten
$^1/_2$ cup water
$^1/_2$ teaspoon salt
2 cups cooked finely mashed pumpkin (butternut
   or flat white pumpkin)
oil for deep-frying

Mix the flour, baking powder and sugar together. Mix the eggs with the water and add the salt. Add this mixture to the dry ingredients and stir through using a wooden spoon until the dough is smooth. Stir in the pumpkin. Heat enough oil for deep-frying in a saucepan. The oil should be hot, but not too hot, otherwise the *vetkoek* will burn on the outside while it's still raw inside. Place spoonfuls of the batter into the oil (two or three at a time, depending on the size of the saucepan). As soon as the *vetkoek* is golden brown and done, remove it using a perforated spoon and place onto a plate and some paper towels to drain the oil. Serve with any filling of your choice or eat as is. You can also make a stuffed *vetkoek* by putting a *frikkadel* (meatball) or piece of cooked sausage in the middle of a spoonful of batter and deep-frying it.

Portuguese bread rolls

Serves 6–8

Is there anyone who doesn't like warm, freshly baked bread? Mozambican bread (Pao) is almost as well-known as its prawns and Deuce M beer. These are best eaten on the same day you bake them.

1 x 10 g sachet instant yeast
$^1/_2$ cup lukewarm water to dissolve the yeast
4 cups cake flour (plus extra to sprinkle over the rolls)
1 teaspoon salt
$^1/_2$ tablespoon sugar
1 tablespoon butter
±1 cup lukewarm water to make the dough

Mix the yeast and the $^1/_2$ cup lukewarm water and set aside for 10 minutes until it starts foaming. Place the flour, salt, sugar and butter in a mixing bowl. Rub the butter into the dry ingredients. Stir in the yeast. Add the remaining lukewarm water bit by bit. Be careful not to add too much – the dough should not be too dry nor too wet. Knead the dough for 10 minutes until it becomes elastic. Place the dough into a bowl, cover with cling wrap and then cover with a large, clean kitchen cloth. Leave it in a warm spot for 1–1$^1/_2$ hours until the dough has doubled in size. Divide the dough into six to eight portions, form round rolls with each, flatten them slightly with your hand and sprinkle flour over. Leave the rolls to rise again until they have doubled in size. Bake on a grid over medium coals for about 30 minutes, turning every now and then.

Desserts

Bread pudding
Serves 10

The sweet layer in this bread pudding makes it something really special. Ensure the pot is not too full, otherwise the sauce will boil over.

Pudding
4 cups full-cream long-life milk
1 cup white sugar
1 heaped tablespoon butter
a pinch of salt
4 eggs, beaten
10 slices white bread, crusts
   removed, cut into blocks

Sweet layer
1 cup soft butter
2 cups sugar
2 eggs

For the pudding: Combine the milk, sugar, butter and salt in a black flat-bottomed pot and heat until the sugar and butter have melted. Add the eggs a little at a time to the warm milk mixture, stirring continuously. Add the bread and stir. Remove from the heat and set aside for 10 minutes so that the bread can soak up the milk. Put the pot over medium coals and place a few coals on the lid. Bake for about 30 minutes or until the pudding has set. Move the pot off the coals, clear the coals from the lid and remove the lid. Put the hot lid out of harm's way.

For the sweet layer: Mix all the ingredients together and spread the mixture over the bread pudding. Put the pot back onto the fire, replace the lid and heap red-hot coals over it so that the upper layer can bake to a dark brown. The coals under the pot must be medium-hot, to prevent the pudding from burning at the bottom. Finally, bake the pudding for another 30 minutes. Eat as is, or with custard.

Tip: The ingredients are enough for a standard black flat-bottomed pot. If you want to use a smaller pot, like a cast-iron bread pan, simply halve the ingredients.

Brown pudding

Serves 8–10

Let's be honest, a brown pudding made in a black flat-bottomed pot tastes just like a pudding baked in the oven. And that's all that matters – scrumptious food, prepared as easily as possible!

Pudding
2 eggs
1 tablespoon butter, melted
1 tablespoon golden syrup
2 cups cake flour
1 teaspoon baking powder
a pinch of salt
1 teaspoon bicarbonate of soda
$^1/_2$ cup milk

Sauce
5 cups water
1 teaspoon vanilla essence
4 cups sugar

For the pudding: Whisk the eggs with a fork in a medium-size bowl. Add the melted butter and syrup and mix well. Stir in the flour, baking powder and salt. Dissolve the bicarbonate of soda in the milk and add to the mixture.

For the sauce: Bring all the sauce ingredients to the boil in a black flat-bottomed pot. Stir until the sugar has dissolved and then move the pot over moderate coals. Place spoonfuls of dough into the sauce and cover. Simmer for 1 hour over low heat without lifting the lid. The pudding goes beautifully brown in the pot and tastes divine with custard or Ideal milk.

African trifle

Serves 4–6

This trifle has the added unique South African flavour of Amarula liqueur.

1 x shop-bought swiss roll, preferably with strawberry jam
$^1/_2$ cup Amarula liqueur
2 cups pecan nuts, roughly chopped
1 x 250 g tub mascarpone cheese
1 x 80 g packet red jelly, any flavour, made according to the packet instructions and set in the fridge
1 cup canned peach slices
1 x 500 ml container long-life custard
$^1/_2$ cup glace cherries, quartered

Cut the Swiss roll into thick slices and place the slices in the bottom of a serving bowl. Drizzle the Amarula liqueur over and let it rest for five minutes to soak in. Sprinkle half the nuts over and spread evenly. Spread a thick layer of the mascarpone cheese over the cake. Break the jelly into loose chunks by dragging a fork over it and spoon the chunks over the cheese. Arrange the peach slices on top and cover with custard. Scatter the cherries and the remaining nuts over the trifle and refrigerate. Serve well chilled.

Tip: To ensure that it looks good too, serve the trifle in a pretty glass bowl (or real glasses that you've carted along to the bush for Christmas). Pack glasses and other breakables in bubble wrap to protect them.

Date squares
Makes about 20 squares

You need something sweet for the road. These date squares have an added ingredient that renews this old recipe: cranberries.

250 g butter
1 cup sugar
2 x 250 g packets pitted dates, finely chopped
1 egg, beaten
$^1/_2$ cup glace cherries, finely chopped
$^1/_2$ cup cranberries
$^1/_2$ cup pecan nuts or almonds, finely chopped
1$^1/_2$ packets (200 g) Marie or Eet-Sum-Mor biscuits,
   broken into rough chunks (place in a plastic bag
   and use a clean bottle or can to crush)
desiccated coconut to sprinkle

Grease a 32 cm x 22 cm pan with butter or nonstick cooking spray. Heat the butter and sugar over medium heat and stir until the sugar has dissolved. Reduce the heat, add the dates and egg, and mix vigorously. Stir in the cherries, cranberries, nuts and biscuit bits and remove from the stove. Pour the mixture into the pan and press down firmly. Sprinkle a little bit of coconut over (not too much otherwise it will be difficult to eat without messing), and leave to cool completely. Cut into squares and store in an airtight container.

Frozen banana
Serves 2

Who would have thought that an ordinary banana could taste like ice cream after it's been frozen?

1 ripe, firm banana, peeled and halved
2 ice-cream sticks
cling wrap

Put an ice-cream stick in each banana half and wrap it in cling wrap. Place in the freezer until frozen.

Peanut butter apple slices
Serves 2

This recipe is incredibly healthy and easy to make.

2 apples, cored and thickly sliced
2 tablespoons peanut butter
$^1/_4$ cup muesli or other breakfast cereal

Spread peanut butter on each apple slice and sprinkle over some muesli.

Pumpkin pudding

Serves 6

Do you remember your Granny's to-die-for roly-poly pudding with its crispy crust and sweet sauce? The one you kept on eating and eating ... Add a soft layer of pumpkin to make it even more delicious.

Pudding
2 cups cake flour
2 tablespoons baking powder
a pinch of salt
$^1/_2$ cup cold butter, cubed
2 eggs, beaten
milk, if required
1 cup cooked mashed pumpkin

$^1/_2$ cup sugar
ground cinnamon

Syrup
2 cups boiling water
1 cup white sugar
2 tablespoons butter

For the pudding: Mix the cake flour, baking powder and salt together. Rub the butter into the flour mixture until it looks like breadcrumbs. Stir in the eggs and mix until the dough is stiff enough so you can roll it out easily. (If the dough is too dry add a little milk.) Roll out the dough into a large rectangle. Spread the cooked pumpkin over the dough, but not all the way to the edges, otherwise it'll spill out. Sprinkle with sugar and cinnamon and carefully roll up the dough from a short end. Seal off the edges by pressing them together. Place the roll in a flat-bottomed cast-iron pot.

For the syrup: Mix the ingredients for the syrup together and stir until the butter has melted. Carefully pour the syrup over the roll. Bake the pudding for 1 hour over moderate coals with a few coals on the lid. Beware of too much heat, and remove the lid after 45 minutes to check as the sauce tends to turn into treacle if things get too hot. You can also bake it in an oven preheated to 180 °C. Serve the pudding lukewarm with cream.

Variation: Instead of baking the roll whole, you can cut it into slices. Place the slices into the pot and pour the syrup over before baking it. It will bake a little faster than when you make one large roll.

Milk tart (filling)

Serves 6

Who can say no to a sweet milk-based cinnamon extravaganza? And served in a pancake, it's twice as nice.

1 x 385 g can condensed milk
3 cups milk
$^1/_4$ cup cornflour
2 eggs
a pinch of salt
1 teaspoon vanilla essence
2 tablespoons butter
$^1/_4$ cup cinnamon sugar (mix together ground cinnamon
    and white sugar to make cinnamon sugar)

Heat the condensed milk and 2 cups of the milk in a pot until it starts simmering. In a separate bowl, mix the rest of the milk with the cornflour until it's smooth. Add the cornflour mixture to the condensed milk mixture and whisk to prevent lumps from forming. Beat the eggs in a separate container and add them a little at a time to the warm milk while stirring continuously. Simmer over low heat for 2–3 minutes. Add the salt, vanilla essence and butter and stir until the butter has melted. Spoon into a serving bowl or individual bowls or into a pancake as a filling, and sprinkle over some cinnamon sugar.

Melkkos

Serves 10

Ask anyone who attended the 'Bekker Landbou' school and they will tell you that this is the tastiest melkkos recipe in the world! The recipe can easily be halved for a smaller safari group.

2 cups butter
$3^1/_2$ cups cake flour
8 cups (2 litres) full-cream long-life milk
$^1/_2$ cup sugar
a pinch of salt
cinnamon sugar to taste

Rub the butter into the cake flour until pea-sized crumbs form. Bring the milk, sugar and salt to the boil in a pot. Lightly stir the flour mixture into the milk with a fork. Don't over stir; the flour mixture should remain coarse. Allow the mixture to simmer over low heat for 10–15 minutes. Sprinkle over cinnamon sugar and serve.

Peppermint Crisp tart
Serves 6–8

Make this easy tart a day in advance and refrigerate to ensure that the biscuits are soft and that the filling has enough time to set.

1 x 250 ml container long-life cream
1 x 360 g can Nestlé Caramel Treat®
1 x 200 g packet Tennis biscuits
1 Peppermint Crisp® chocolate, grated

Beat the cream until stiff peaks form. Place half of the cream into a different bowl and set aside. Stir the remaining cream into the Caramel Treat® until well mixed. Pack a layer of Tennis biscuits into the bottom of a square dish and spread a third of the caramel filling onto the biscuits. Carry on layering until all the ingredients are used up. Depending on the size of the dish, you'll have three layers. (If you're making the tart in a plastic container with a lid, it's easy to stow in the fridge.) Use the rest of the cream to cover the tart and sprinkle the Peppermint Crisp over it.

Variation: If someone in your group doesn't like peppermint, serve the grated chocolate in a separate bowl so every person can sprinkle some on top of his or her serving. The tart is tasty on its own as well.

Chocolate cake in oranges

Serves 6

This recipe might sound like a gimmick (who has heard of an orange being used as a cake pan?), but it tastes first-class. The orange halves lend a special flavour to the chocolate cake. Moreover, it is, 'a piece of cake' to make.

6 oranges
1 x 510 g packet Pillsbury Rich Chocolate Cake® mix
2 eggs
1¼ cups water
⅓ cup oil
foil (enough for 6 parcels)
icing sugar
cherries (optional)

Cut off the upper part of the orange, big enough so that you can insert a knife and a spoon into the hole to remove the flesh. Using a sharp knife, loosen the flesh in a circular motion, then scoop it out with a spoon without damaging the peel. (Keep the orange segments for a salad.) Mix the cake mixture, eggs, water and oil together and spoon the mixture into the orange cups. Only half-fill the oranges with the cake mixture. Place the orange lids on top of the oranges and wrap up each orange firmly in a double-layer of foil. Place the parcels upright on the grid over low to medium-hot coals for 30 minutes. Open one orange to test whether the cake has cooked before removing all of them from the grid (push a sharp knife into the centre of the cake; it should come out clean). Leave the cake to cool slightly then sprinkle with icing sugar. You can put a cherry on top to round it off.

Boarding school pudding

Serves 8

Many kids grew up with this pudding, especially those who attended boarding school. Many variations exist – you can use different biscuits or sprinkle nuts on top.

1 x 500 ml container long-life custard
1 x 200 g packet Marie biscuits
½ cup apricot jam or Nestlé Caramel Treat®
chocolate sticks or crumbed chocolate to decorate

Heat the custard in a small saucepan until very hot. Join the biscuits in pairs by spreading the apricot jam or Caramel Treat® over one biscuit and sticking a second biscuit on top. Place the biscuit sandwiches in a flat dish that is large enough for two or three rows of biscuits. You can also make individual servings. Pour the hot custard over the first layer of biscuits, pack another layer of biscuits on top and pour over the rest of the custard. Let the pudding stand for 30 minutes to allow the biscuits to soften before serving. Decorate with chocolate sticks or grated chocolate.

Rice dumplings

Serves 6

Not everyone likes traditional rice pudding and this recipe is a good alternative.

2 cups cooked rice
1 cup cake flour
2 teaspoons baking powder
1 teaspoon salt
2 eggs, beaten
$^1/_4$ cup cinnamon sugar
2 tablespoons butter, melted

Fill a pot halfway with warm water, place on the stove and bring to a simmer. Mix together all the ingredients, except the melted butter and cinnamon sugar. Carefully place tablespoonfuls of the mixture into the water but don't place more than four tablespoonsful into the pot at a time. Place the lid on top and simmer for 10 minutes at a time. Place the cooked dumplings in a serving bowl, sprinkle over cinnamon sugar and drip butter over the dumplings. Cover the serving bowl with a lid while the other dumplings are cooking to keep the dumplings warm. Repeat the above process until the mixture is finished and all the dumplings have been cooked.

Quick ice cream

Serves 1

If you are not craving ice cream by day nine of the safari then you'll never crave it again.

$^1/_2$ cup milk
1 tablespoon icing sugar
$^1/_4$ teaspoon vanilla essence (or any other flavour)

Place all the ingredients in a small Ziploc® bag, squeeze out the air and seal. Shake the bag to mix the ingredients and dissolve the sugar. Place the packet in the freezer. Remove it as soon as it starts freezing. Finely crush the ice crystals and put it back in the freezer until the ice cream is frozen. Serve in a bowl or in a ice-cream cone.

Fruit ice-lollies

Serves 10

These ice-lollies are easy to make and your biggest concern should be stopping the adults from eating all the kid's ice-lollies.

4 cups water
$1^1/_2$ cups sugar
2 cups fresh fruit juice
plastic containers (that you can use to mould the
  ice-lollies)

Boil the water and add the sugar. Stir until the sugar has dissolved. Add the fruit juice and set aside to cool. Pour the fruit juice into plastic containers and place in the freezer until completely frozen.

Index

African trifle 146
apple rings, Sausage with 83
apple slices, Peanut
    butter 149
asparagus, Fried haloumi
    and 104
Avocado ritz 121

bacon-and-egg salad,
    Easy 128
Banana
    chips, wild 135
    frozen 149
bean stew, Cape Malay 64
Béchamel sauce 87
Beef
    biltong-and-pasta
        salad 121
    bully beef and eggs 11
    chakalaka cottage pie 53
    chilli con carne 55
    curry meatballs 59
    Madras 51
    meat pie in a braai grid 80
    Moroccan mince 76
    Portuguese espetadas 67
    salad of roast figs and
        biltong 125
    silverside and potatoes 52
    steak stir-fry 75
    sweet-and-sour
        boerewors 72
    tomato stew 79
    Zorba's moussaka 87
Beef Madras 51

Biltong
    and-pasta salad 121
    salad of roast figs and
        biltong 125
Blue cheese salad 122
Boarding school pudding 155
Bobotie
    fish 33
    ostrich 84
boerewors, Sweet-and
    -sour 72
Boiled bush omelette 21
Braai sauce 89
Bread
    and-tomato salad 122
    basic recipe 137
    health loaf 141
    Portuguese rolls 142
    pudding 145
    raisin 141
    wheels 12
Brown pudding 146
Bully beef and eggs 11
Burgers
    chickpea 107
    ostrich, easy 63
Butter chicken 37
Butternut and tomato
    soup 27

Calamari rings 29
Cape Malay bean stew 64
caramel sauce, Easy 93
Caramelised onions 15
Chakalaka cottage pie 53

Cheese scones in a jaffle
    pan 138
Chicken
    and lentil curry 38
    butter 37
    cola 42
    Hawaiian pizzas 39
    livers 41
    meatballs 41
    orange-and-chicken
        potato salad 126
    paella 45
    peri-peri butterfly 46
    potjie 42
    with tequila and
        cinnamon 49
    salad, cold 125
    stew, fragrant 37
Chickpea
    burgers 107
    stew 107
Chilli con carne 55
chips, Wild banana 135
Chocolate
    cake in oranges 155
    sauce 93
Coconut rice 131
cottage pie, Chakalaka 53
Couscous 132
Couscous salad 126
Curry
    beef Madras 51
    chicken and lentil 38
    eggs 108
    meatballs 59

rogan josh lamb 68
vegetarian 108

Date squares 149
dumplings, Rice 156

Eggs
    bacon-and-eggs salad,
        easy 128
    bully beef and 11
    curry 108
    frittata 15
    in a hole 12
    Mexican 19
    omelette, boiled bush 21
    poached, in cling wrap 21
    scotch 20
    snacks 131
espetadas, Portuguese 67

figs, and biltong salad 125
Fish (see also Seafood)
    balls 34
    bobotie 33
    stew 30
    snoek on an open fire 34
    trout spread 29
Fried haloumi and
    asparagus 104
Frittata 15
Fritters
    mealie 112
    pumpkin 115
Frozen banana 149
Fruit ice-lollies 156

gazpacho, Watermelon 24
gravy, Easy 89
Greek leg of lamb 56
Green pumpkin peel 116

haloumi and asparagus,
    Fried 104
Hawaiian chicken pizzas 38
Health loaf 141
honey-mustard marinade 83

ice cream, Quick 156
ice-lollies, Fruit 156
Italian meatballs 60

Kebabs
    Granny's sosaties 64
    tortillas 75
    watermelon 128
kleftiko, Lamb 63

Lamb
    Granny's sosaties
        (kebabs) 64
    Greek leg of 56
    in a pot, leg of 71
    kleftiko 63
    ribs, sticky 55
    rogan josh 68
lasagna, Pumpkin 99
Leg of lamb in a pot 71
lentil curry, Chicken
    and 38
livers, Chicken 41

Macaroni milk pudding 95
Madras, Beef 51
Marinade
    honey-mustard 83

Mealie
    fritters 112
    on the coals 115
Meat pie in a braai grid 80
Meatballs
    chicken 41
    curry 59
    Italian 60
Melkkos 151
Mexican eggs 19
Milk
    pudding, macaroni 95
    tart (filling) 151
    mince, Moroccan 76
    moussaka, Zorba's 87

omelette, Boiled bush 21
Onions
    caramelised 15
    rings 119
Orange-and-chicken potato
    salad 126
oranges, Chocolate cake
    in 155
Ostrich
    burgers, easy 63
    bobotie 84
    steak strips on pasta 100
    steaks with honey-
        mustard marinade 83
Oxtail stew 51

Paella 45
pancake batter, Basic 138
Pasta
    and ragu meat sauce 96
    lasagna, pumpkin 99
    macaroni milk pudding 95
    ostrich steak strips on 100

rasta pasta 96
salad, colourful pasta 95
sausages, worm 100
Pea soup 23
Peanut butter apple
    slices 149
Pepper sauce 90
Peppermint Crisp tart 152
peppers, Stuffed 103
Peri-peri butterfly chicken 46
pesto, Potatoes with 111
Pie
    chakalaka cottage 53
    meat, in a braai grid 80
pizzas, Hawaiian chicken 39
Poached egg in
    cling wrap 21
Pork
    bacon-and-egg, easy
        salad 128
    Italian meatballs 60
    ribs, sticky 55
    sweet-and-sour stew 72
Portuguese
    bread rolls 142
    espetadas 67
    potato, salad Orange-and-
        -chicken,126
Potatoes
    silverside and 52
    volcano 119
    with lemon zest 111
    with pesto 111
potjie, Chicken 42
prawn soup, Easy 24
Pudding
    African trifle 146
    boarding school 155
    bread 145

brown 146
chocolate cake in
    oranges 155
macaroni milk 95
melkkos 151
milk tart (filling) 151
peppermint crisp tart 152
pumpkin 150
rice dumplings 156
Pumpkin
    fritters 115
    green peel 116
    lasagna 99
    pudding 150
    stew 67
    tomato 118
    vetkoek 142

Quiche in a tin cup 11

ragu meat sauce, Pasta
    and 96
Raisin bread 141
Rasta pasta 96
ribs, Sticky 55
Rice
    coconut 131
    dumplings 156
    salad with fruit 129
    tomato rice, from West
        Africa 135
    traditional yellow 132
Rogan josh lamb curry 68

Salad
    avocado ritz 121
    biltong-and-pasta 121
    blue cheese 122
    bread-and-tomato 122

chicken, cold 125
pasta, colourful 95
couscous 126
bacon-and-egg, easy 128
of roast figs and biltong 125
orange-and-chicken
    potato 126
rice with fruit 129
Sauce
    béchamel 87
    braai 89
    caramel, easy 93
    chocolate 93
    gravy, easy 89
    pepper 90
    sweet-and-sour 90
    white 99
Sausage
    stew 16
    sweet-and-sour
        boerewors 72
    with apple rings 83
    worm 100
scones, Cheese in a jaffle
    pan 138

Scotch eggs 20
Seafood
    calamari rings 29
    prawn soup, easy 24
Silverside and potatoes 52
Snoek on an open fire 34
Sosatie
    Granny's (kebabs) 64
Soup
    butternut and tomato 27
    pea 23
    prawn, easy 24
    sweet potato 27
spread, Trout 29
Steak
    Ostrich steak strips on
        pasta 100
    Ostrich with honey-
        mustard marinade 83
    stir-fry 75
Stew
    Cape Malay bean 64
    chicken, fragrant 37
    chickpea 107
    fish 30

oxtail 51
pumpkin 67
sausage 16
sweet-and-sour pork 72
tomato 79
stir-fry, Steak 75
Stuffed peppers 103
Sweet-and-sour boerewors 72
Sweet-and-sour pork
    stew 72
Sweet-and-soursauce 90
Sweet potato
    and-spinach filling 122
    soup 27
    with cream cheese 116
Sweet snacks
    date squares 149
    frozen banana 149
    fruit ice-lollies 156
    peanut butter apple
        slices 149
    quick ice cream 156

Tart
    Milk 151

Peppermint Crisp 152
Tomato
    bread-and-tomato salad 122
    butternut and tomato
        soup 27
    pumpkin and tomato 118
    rice from West Africa 135
    stew 79
    tortillas, Kebab 75
Traditional yellow rice 132
trifle, African 146
Trout spread 29

Vegetarian curry 108
vetkoek, Pumpkin 142
Volcano potatoes 119

Watermelon
    kebabs 128
    gazpacho 24
White sauce 99
Wild banana chips 135
Worm sausages 100

Zorba's moussaka 87

Conversion Table

TEASPOONS

Metric	Imperial
2 ml	$1/4$ tsp
3 ml	$1/2$ tsp
5 ml	1 tsp
10 ml	2 tsp
20 ml	4 tsp

TABLESPOONS

Metric	Imperial
15 ml	1 Tbsp
30 ml	2 Tbsp
45 ml	3 Tbsp

CUPS

Metric	Imperial
60 ml	$1/4$ cup
80 ml	$1/3$ cup
125 ml	$1/2$ cup
160 ml	$2/3$ cup
200 ml	$3/4$ cup
250 ml	1 cup
375 ml	$1 1/2$ cups
500 ml	2 cups
1 litre	4 cups